THe Power of a Positive Wife

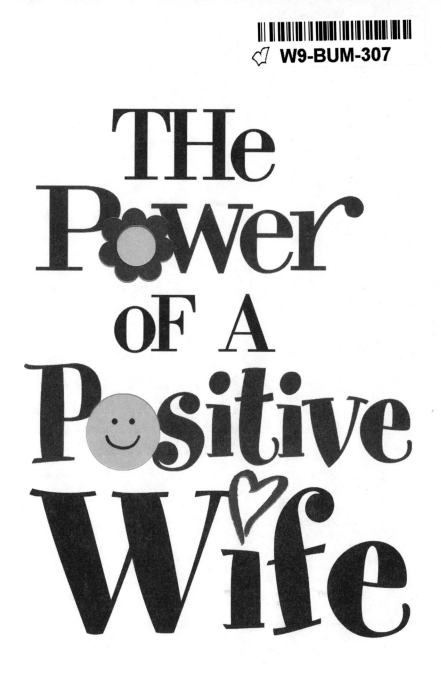

About the Author

Best selling author **Karol Ladd** offers lasting hope and biblical truth to women around the world through her positive book series. A gifted communicator and dynamic leader, Karol is founder and president of Positive Life Principles, Inc., a resource company offering strategies for success in both home and work. Her vivacious personality makes her a popular speaker to women's organizations, church groups and corporate events. She is co-founder of a character-building club for young girls called USA Sonshine Girls and serves on several educational boards. Karol is a frequent guest on radio and television programs. Her most valued role is that of wife to Curt and mother to daughters Grace and Joy. Visit her Web site at PositiveLifePrinciples.com.

Other books by Karol Ladd

The Power of a Positive Mom

The Power of a Positive Woman

Scream Savers, Calming Ideas for Frazzled Moms

Table Talk

Fun House

Summer with a Smile

The Glad Scientist Series

THe Power OF A Positive Wife

Karol Ladd

HOWARD
PUBLISHING CO.

Our purpose at Howard Publishing is to:
- *Increase faith* in the hearts of growing Christians
- *Inspire holiness* in the lives of believers
- *Instill hope* in the hearts of struggling people everywhere

Because He's coming again!

The Power of a Positive Wife © 2003 by Karol Ladd
All rights reserved. Printed in the United States of America

Published by Howard Publishing Co., Inc.,
3117 North 7th Street, West Monroe, Louisiana 71291-2227

04 05 06 07 08 09 10 11 12   10 9 8 7 6 5 4 3

Edited by Michele Buckingham
Interior design by John Luke
Cover design by LinDee Loveland

ISBN: 1-58229-306-6

Some of the names used in the stories in this book are not the actual names; identifying details have been changed to protect anonymity. Any resemblance is purely coincidental.

Contents

Contents

Acknowledgments

A heartfelt thanks to Dr. Deborah Newman, Carol Floch, Amy Reppert, and Leslie Hodge for the sound advice and wise input you gave to the contents of this book. You are tremendous blessings to my life.

Thanks also to Susan, Beth, Terry Ann, Dana, and Jane for the support and ideas you added to this book. You are truly positive friends.

My sincere gratitude to the tremendous team at Howard Publishing, and especially my extraordinary editors, Philis Boultinghouse and Michele Buckingham.

My greatest thanks to my wonderful husband, Curt; companion, encourager, leader, and supporter. I love you. You are a gift from God.

Most importantly, thanks be to God who gives us the strength and power to be positive wives moment by moment.

There is no more lovely, friendly, and charming relationship, communion, or company than a good marriage.

—Martin Luther

Introduction

The Influence of a Positive Wife
The Choice Is Yours

A worthy wife is her husband's joy and crown.

—Proverbs 12:4 TLB

Let me guess. When you first got married, you fully intended to be a positive wife. It was your desire to be uplifting and supportive from the moment you blissfully uttered your marriage vows and promised "until death do us part." But somewhere between the honeymoon and the happily ever after, you found yourself struggling to be the poster child for affirmative spouses. Your responsibilities increased. Your husband's attentiveness waned. And suddenly you weren't the wonderfully positive wife you always thought you'd be.

Me too! At my wedding I had the blissful picture in my mind of lovingly greeting my husband at the door each evening (looking like I just stepped off the cover of a fashion magazine, of course), kissing him on the cheek, and thanking him for the flowers he'd sent me. We would magically sit down to a delicious, home-cooked meal, gaze into each other's eyes, and intimately share the details of our day.

Oddly enough, it hasn't played out that way at our house. How about at yours? If I'm gazing into my husband's eyes, it's probably because I'm trying to get him to help with the kids or take out the

Introduction

garbage. And a home-cooked dinner? Well, let's move on to another subject.

This book is all about recapturing that spark of encouragement and joy we once envisioned for our marriages. It's about being positive wives (not perfect ones) and building stronger and healthier marriages in the process. Each of us has the opportunity to move our marriages in a positive direction, even in the midst of challenges or disappointments. The powerful principles provided in these pages can help us develop deeper, more meaningful relationships with our husbands as we apply them to our lives.

With confidence I call these principles *powerful,* not because they come from me, but because they come from God's Word. The seven principles for being a positive wife are constructed on the sure foundation of truth found in the Bible. You will see that these timeless and practical principles can be applied to any marriage, including yours— whether you're happy and at peace or struggling to survive. This book is written to give you a lift and a boost of encouragement. My aim is to come alongside you and help you deepen the joy and experience the possibilities that your marriage offers, no matter what state it is in right now.

You can read this book for your own personal growth and enrichment, or you can use it in a group study with the women in your church or community. The Power Points at the end of each chapter offer scriptures to read with questions to ponder, sample prayers to pray, verses to memorize, and activities to help you effectively put the principles of the chapter into practice. Don't skip the Power Points! Reading a book is beneficial; but applying its content to our lives is what makes the information valuable not only to us, but also to the people around us.

Perhaps you're thinking, *But you don't know me. I'm just a negative sort of person. There's no way I can be a positive wife.* The question is, can any woman (and I mean *any* woman) be a positive wife? Yes! How do I know? Because with God, all things are possible. God is a God of hope and power. He is at work in our lives, and he has given us his Spirit to help us live out the principles in his Word. The Book of Romans offers a word of encouragement for every believer, and especially for every wife: "May the God of hope fill you with all joy and peace as you trust in him, so that you may overflow with hope by the power of the Holy Spirit" (Romans 15:13).

Yes, a positive wife chooses to put her hope in God. She does not look to her husband or her circumstances to fill her with joy and contentment; she looks to her heavenly Father. It's God's power that allows her to be a wife of love, commitment, encouragement, and respect. It's his work that gives her beauty inside out, helps her live responsibly, and develops a godly spirit within her.

God can take each of us where we are right now (mess that we may be) and form and fashion us into wonderful complements and glowing crowns for our husbands. Believe it! He can make us positive wives who have great influence in our homes through the positive tone we set. Our words, attitudes, and actions can have a powerful impact for good in our marriages and our families.

Do I have a picture-perfect marriage? Let me set the record straight: My marriage is strong, but it is not void of challenges or its fair share of differences of opinion. The truth is, no one has a perfect situation at home. How do I know? Because there are no perfect people. Everyone has flaws, weaknesses, and faults. That includes my husband and me—and your husband and you. Whenever two sinful people are meshed together in marriage, they will experience challenges along the

When you make the sacrifice in marriage, you're sacrificing not to each other but to unity in a relationship.

—Joseph Campbell

☺

3

way. The question is, how will we choose to handle those challenges? Will we learn to respond in a positive and healing way, or will we use our words and actions in a destructive and negative way?

The main purpose of this book is not to make your marriage better, although most likely that will be a result. The main purpose is to help you become a positive influence in your marriage (no matter what your husband is like). It is meant to facilitate your efforts to be the woman and the wife God has created you to be. Think of it as a vitamin boost to nourish your spiritual, physical, mental, and emotional growth. Within these pages you will find encouragement to help you grow in your commitment and love for your husband. You will find helpful hints on the art of arguing and the gift of forgiving. You'll find practical suggestions on how to respect and honor your husband with your words and actions, as well as terrific tips for enhancing the physical attraction between you. Great date ideas, wonderful ways to maintain your home, and advice on handling financial responsibilities are all a part of this positive-wife portfolio.

Whether you take the ideas in this book in small doses or gulp them down all at once, I think you'll find that *The Power of a Positive Wife* will give you practical principles for positive living that cannot help but strengthen your relationship with your spouse. Author Neil Clark Warren said, "Great marriages seldom come naturally. They are virtually always the result of strong motivation, careful instruction, and endless practice."[1] My hope is that as you read this book, you will be boosted by the strong motivation and careful instruction provided in each chapter.

The endless practice will be up to you!

THe ImPacT OF A Positive Wife

*A wife of noble character who can find? She is worth
far more than rubies.*

—Proverbs 31:10

The man [Adam] said, "This is now bone of my bones and flesh of my flesh; she shall be called 'woman,' for she was taken out of man." For this reason a man will leave his father and mother and be united to his wife, and they will become one flesh.

—Genesis 2:23–24

Wifeology
The Study of Being a Great Wife

Marriage is the greatest institution ever invented! It can be good, or it can be great, but it should never be ordinary.

—Neil Clark Warren

Here's a little word quiz.

Do you know what the following "-ologies" refer to?

- Rhinology
- Speleology
- Vexillology
- Campanology
- Oology

You may be surprised, as I was, to find out that *rhinology* is not the study of rhinoceroses, but rather the study of the nose. And while it's tempting to think that *speleology* has something to do with the study of your child's spelling list, it's really the study of caves. *Vexillology* is not the study of angry women; it's actually the study of flags. (*Vexillum* is the Latin word for flag.) *Campanology* doesn't have anything to do with camping; it's the study of bell ringing. (Are there really campanologists out there?) And of course, *oology* is the study of what audiences say at the circus. Just kidding! It's really the study of bird eggs.[1]

For the purpose of this book, I have invented a new "ology." It's *wifeology*, the study of being a great wife. Not just a mediocre wife or one who simply survives her marriage, but a wonderful wife. You won't find an official wifeology course in a high-school or college catalog; nonetheless, it is one of the most important studies a wife can pursue.

If you could choose the one ingredient that makes a great wife, what would it be? Is a woman considered a wonderful wife if she's totally focused on the needs of her husband? If her every waking moment is motivated by the underlying question "What can I do to make my husband's world a better place?" Granted, most husbands would love this attention; but honestly, that's not the key ingredient to wifely success. Is it being a great sex partner or a thrifty spender or a good organizer of the home? These are nice qualities, but again, they aren't the most important thing.

This may shock you, but the one essential, foundational principle for being a great wife doesn't have anything to do with the husband. Does this statement surprise you? It's true. You might naturally think that wifeology is all about making a husband happy and content, but these are simply the beneficial results of a woman who practices wifeology.

So, are you ready? Here it is: The most important ingredient in the recipe for a great wife is God-centeredness (not husband-centeredness). First and foremost, a great wife is a godly woman. Not necessarily a church lady or a Bible-study attendee or even a prayer-circle leader. All of these are good things to be, but a godly woman has the distinct characteristic of having a deep and vibrant love relationship with God. She is a woman who loves the Lord, her God, with all her heart, mind, soul, and strength.

Why does a godly woman make a great wife? Let's examine the blessings that overflow from her life.

A godly wife forgives, loves, serves, and encourages her husband as a natural outpouring of her love and devotion to her heavenly Father. She isn't demanding, controlling, or overbearing, because she walks in God's grace and offers that grace freely to her husband and others. She reflects the positive qualities of the fruit of the Spirit: love, joy, peace, patience, kindness, goodness, faithfulness, gentleness, and self-control.

Her walk with God allows her to keep the other areas of her life in balance. She doesn't sweat the small stuff, but focuses on things of eternal value. Nor does she live on a performance track, trying to please her husband in order to gain his approval. She looks to God, not her husband, for affirmation and acceptance. A God-centered wife enjoys her relationship with her husband, understanding that both husband and wife are God-given complements to one another. She finds her joy, peace, and inner strength from the only true source: God himself.

You may be thinking, *Come on. No one is that perfect!* You're right. No one is—but that's the great thing about God's redemptive power. God is in the business of taking weak, ordinary, sinful creatures; redeeming them; and changing them into beautiful new creations. His power and work in our lives make us better than we could ever hope to be on our own.

A Beautiful Beginning

Let's begin our wifeology study by taking a look back in history. In the first two chapters of the Book of Genesis, we read that all things were created by God, and they were all declared good. All, that is, except one: It was not good that man was alone. You would think that God and man living in fellowship and harmony in the wonder of the newly created Garden of Eden would be a great thing. But no, it was not good. God knew that man needed a helper—a complement to his masculine traits. So he fashioned and designed a female as that perfect complement.

In his omniscient plan, God created man and woman as perfect counterparts to one another. Yes, they had similarities, but they also had unique differences. God placed certain, distinct qualities and traits in man and certain, distinct qualities and traits in woman. Together they were designed to function as one flesh. They were to bless each other. They were to encourage each other's strengths and balance each other's weaknesses. They were to take a selfless and loving position in each other's lives.

That plan has never changed. You and I are designed by God to bless, complement, and serve our spouses lovingly and selflessly. How do we do that? Paul offers us a powerful guideline in Philippians 2:3–5: "Do nothing out of selfish ambition or vain conceit, but in humility consider others better than yourselves. Each of you should look not only to your own interests, but also to the interests of others. Your attitude should be the same as that of Christ Jesus." These profound words can—and should—apply to our marriages just as much as they apply to relationships in general. Our objective as Christians is to follow Christ's example and look out for the interests of others—especially our spouses.

In his book *Authentic Faith,* Gary Thomas encourages believers to live beyond themselves. He writes:

> To experience Christ's joy, passion, and fulfillment, we need to adopt an entirely new *mind-set* and *motivation:* We are invited to join our Lord in living for the glory of the Father instead of for our own reputation, and we are called to give ourselves over to the salvation and sanctification of Christ's bride, the church, rather than to be consumed by our own welfare. This holy self-forgetfulness is the most genuine mark of true faith, the evidence of God's merciful grace in our lives.[2]

As wifeologists we need to apply Thomas's words to our marriages. Being a great wife calls us to step out of ourselves, devote ourselves to God, and live out his love for our husbands in a selfless way.

The Wifeologist's Instruction Manual

When I think about instructions for living a positive, God-centered life, Romans 12 comes to mind. In this profound chapter, Paul taught the early Christians how to relate to both God and man—in just twenty-one verses! Let's delve into Romans 12, not only from our perspective as Christians, but more specifically from our position as wives. Paul begins by addressing our relationship to God:

> And so, dear Christian friends, I plead with you to give your bodies to God. Let them be a living and holy sacrifice—the kind he will accept. When you think of what he has done for you, is this too much to ask? Don't copy the behavior and customs of this world, but let God transform you into a new person by changing the way you think. Then you will know what God wants you to do, and you will know how good and pleasing and perfect his will really is. (Romans 12:1–2 NLT)

How wonderful to think that God's will for us is good, pleasing, and perfect. What a great heavenly Father we have! Because God gave his only Son to die on the cross on our behalf, we can willingly give our lives as a living sacrifice to him. Paul encourages us to do just that by changing our way of thinking—by no longer thinking the way the world does (the "what's in it for me?" syndrome) but, rather, allowing God to transform our minds and change our viewpoint to a more eternal one. He continues:

> As God's messenger, I give each of you this warning: Be honest in your estimate of yourselves, measuring your value by how much faith God has given you. Just as our bodies have many parts and

A joyful marriage is a bit of heaven on earth. —Heine

11

each part has a special function, so it is with Christ's body. We are all parts of his one body, and each of us has different work to do. And since we are all one body in Christ, we belong to each other, and each of us needs all the others. (Romans 12:3–5 NLT)

Here Paul is telling us not to think more highly of ourselves than we ought. In today's world it's so easy to let a little voice inside our heads tell us how much we deserve. Be honest. How often have you thought in terms of *But I deserve...* or *I have a right to...*? Don't get me wrong. I'm not saying we should denigrate ourselves or think too little of our calling in life. But as Paul said, we are to have an honest estimation of ourselves based on our faith.

The wonderful thing is that by placing our faith in Christ, we have great worth. Our value is based on the fact that we become a part of God's family when we trust in him. We are royalty—daughters of the King! The apostle John put it this way: "To all who received him, to those who believed in his name, he gave the right to become children of God—children born not of natural descent, nor of human decision or a husband's will, but born of God" (John 1:12–13).

Have you taken that step of placing your faith in Christ? God's plan of salvation is simple. Our wonderful, loving, and perfect heavenly Father provided a way for mankind to be forgiven of sin and have the promise of eternal life. He sacrificially gave his only son, Jesus, to die on the cross on our behalf. Whoever believes in Jesus will not perish but have eternal life (see John 3:16). It's as simple as believing! Perhaps you want to stop reading right now and take a moment to talk to God, placing your faith and trust in his Son, Jesus. Go ahead. I'll wait for you.

As believers, our value doesn't come from how well we perform. It doesn't come from the significant things we accomplish or the awards we win. Paul says our worth is based on our faith. It's based on our recognition that the gifts and talents we have are from God and that

12

without God we are nothing. We should never become prideful concerning our gifts and strengths, but rather use them as a part of the body of Christ to help and encourage others.

Of course, when Paul refers to "one body in Christ," he is talking about Christians in general. Still I can't help but be reminded of Genesis 2:24: "they will become one flesh." In marriage, as in the body of Christ, we are called to bring our gifts and talents together to function as one.

> God has given each of us the ability to do certain things well. So if God has given you the ability to prophesy, speak out when you have faith that God is speaking through you. If your gift is that of serving others, serve them well. If you are a teacher, do a good job of teaching. If your gift is to encourage others, do it! If you have money, share it generously. If God has given you leadership ability, take the responsibility seriously. And if you have a gift for showing kindness to others, do it gladly. (Romans 12:6–8 NLT)

Often when we contemplate marriage, we worry about losing our autonomy and individuality. But "becoming one" doesn't mean losing who we are as individuals; rather, it means *using* who we are as individuals to strengthen the marriage. Marriage is all about two unique individuals working together as one. A husband and wife are like two strands of rope, twined together for greater strength and more useful service. As Solomon said, "Two are better than one, because they have a good return for their work" (Ecclesiastes 4:9).

Who are you? How are you unique? What gifts and talents do you possess? How do your strengths complement your spouse? How do his strengths balance your weaknesses? God uses everything that we are—our strengths; our weaknesses; our gifts, talents, and abilities—to make our marriages everything they ought to be.

In Proverbs 31 we find Solomon's description of a godly and noble wife. Take a moment to open your Bible and read over that chapter. Here we see a picture of a positive woman who enriches her marriage with her unique identity. She doesn't dissolve into the marriage and become invisible. Quite the contrary, God uses her giftedness to make her a crown to her husband and a blessing to her family. May each of us learn to use our gifts for the good of others in our marriages, in our homes, with our children, and within the church!

True Love Isn't for Wimps

In the next few verses of Romans 12, Paul digs deeper into the love we ought to have in our relationships with one another. Let me give you a warning: This passage is not for wimps. Paul is talking here about showing true love, and it ain't easy. He's not talking about "touchy-feely-fluffy" love, like the kind we had in high school or when we felt those first flutters for a boyfriend. He is talking about devoted love. Love that involves a commitment to others. It would be wonderful to see this type of love practiced in our churches today. If our goal is to be great wives, it's essential to see this kind of love practiced in our marriages.

As we read the next few verses, let's take Paul's love challenge. As Christians, it's our responsibility to love. Oddly enough, Paul never mentions that our love is dependent upon whether or not the other person treats us with love first.

Don't just pretend that you love others. Really love them. Hate what is wrong. Stand on the side of the good. Love each other with genuine affection, and take delight in honoring each other. Never be lazy in your work, but serve the Lord enthusiastically. Be glad for all God is planning for you. Be patient in trouble, and always be prayerful....When others are happy, be happy with them. If they are sad, share their sorrow. Live in harmony with each other. Don't try to act important, but enjoy the company of ordinary people. And don't think you know it all! (Romans 12:9–12, 15–16 NLT)

Showing true love means helping others become better people. Let's not look at our husbands and be horrified by their weaknesses. Instead, with eyes of love, let's look past our husband's flaws (recognizing that we have a few flaws ourselves) and enjoy the fact that God has placed us together as harmonious complements to one another. Be patient with your husband and with the difficult times that are inevitable in marriage. Be on the same page with your spouse so that when he is happy, you are happy with him. When he is down, empathize with him.

Never pay back evil for evil to anyone. Do things in such a way that everyone can see you are honorable. Do your part to live in peace with everyone, as much as possible. Dear friends, never avenge yourselves. Leave that to God. For it is written, "I will take vengeance; I will repay those who deserve it," says the Lord. Instead, do what the Scriptures say: "If your enemies are hungry, feed them. If they are thirsty, give them something to drink, and they will be ashamed of what they have done to you." Don't let evil get the best of you, but conquer evil by doing good. (Romans 12:17–21 NLT)

Let's be clear about one thing: This passage is not referring to abusive relationships. There is a time when a wife must stand up, get away, and protect herself and her children from harm. Paul is not talking about abusive situations whatsoever. Rather, he is giving us general life principles concerning all of our relationships. These are core instructions for Christian living that ought to play out in our role as wives and as Christians. Loving others as Christ loved us means being willing to forgive and extend grace, even to those who do not seem to deserve it. Of course, our natural tendency is to want to repay hurt for hurt. But Paul is telling us here that revenge is not our job; it's God's.

As wives, one of our favorite ways to get back at our husbands is to hold a grudge. We give them the silent treatment, throw a temper tantrum, or even withhold sex, thinking, *I'll show him how hurt I am!* Oops! That's exactly what Paul tells us *not* to do! What right do we have to hold a grudge over anyone, since we, too, are recipients of God's grace?

If anyone ever had reason to seek revenge, it was Paul. He was beaten, stoned, and put in prison simply for declaring the gospel of Jesus. He could have said, "No fair!" He could have gotten angry and sought revenge, but he chose, instead, to forgive and move on. And he was probably a happier man for it.

You and I need to practice the profound principle of forgiving and dropping past hurts, not only for the sake of others, but for our own. After all, what do anger, bitterness, and an I'm-going-to-get-you-back attitude do for us? Do they make us better people or just bitter ones? Do they have a positive effect on our relationships or a negative effect?

Of course, choosing not to seek revenge doesn't mean that we become doormats. Not at all! Practicing the principles in Romans 12 is actually a sign of strength. It takes strength of character to forgive and not hold a grudge. It takes strength not to lower ourselves by paying back evil for evil or playing foolish games, but instead, living honorably, doing our part to preserve peace. There is a wise way to handle every conflict, as we will learn in chapter 6. There are also times to take a firm moral stand. But we must relinquish to the Lord the desire to "get back" at others—including our husbands.

Forgiveness is a key element in any relationship, but it's especially important in a marriage relationship. We'll delve further into the nitty-gritty of forgiveness in chapter 4.

The Beauty of Our Differences

Wouldn't marriage be easier if husbands and wives were exactly alike? If we saw eye to eye on every issue? If we were on the same page with every decision? We'd have nothing to argue about! But if we had no contradictions between us, no checks and balances, no disagreements or second opinions, then I dare say we would find ourselves making bigger mistakes faster in our lives. Oddly enough, tension can be a good thing. It is resistance that builds muscle. We need each other—and the friction caused by our differences—to grow strong.

Reflect for a moment on all the complementary items we use each day: nuts and bolts, cup and saucer, hammer and nails, needle and thread, fork and knife, soap and water. Each couplet represents two separate, individual objects working together to help and complete each other. We need to see our marriages in a similar light—as two individuals working together for a greater good, not working against each other simply because we have differences. Sinclair Ferguson said, "Marriage, and the process of coming to it, is not heaven! It is the bonding together of two needy sinners in order to make a partnership that is substantially greater than either of them alone."[3]

The Powerful Influence of a Wife

Wives were created by God for a significant plan and purpose. The Genesis account makes clear that Creation wasn't complete until the wife was brought on the scene. That means that you and I have a powerful and important place in this world. As wives we have an awesome influence, and with that comes an incredible responsibility. With our influence we have the power to become a crown to our husbands or a thorn in their sides. Proverbs 12:4 says, "A worthy wife is her husband's joy and crown; a shameful wife saps his strength" (NLT). In other words, we can choose to be joy givers or joy zappers. We can be positive or

17

negative, a blessing or a curse. We can build our husbands up to be kings, or we can wear them down with bitterness, whining, and anger. We set the tone for our homes. Proverbs 19:13–14 says that "a nagging wife annoys like a constant dripping…but only the LORD can give an understanding wife" (NLT).

The story is told of a young girl who was attending a wedding ceremony for the first time. She leaned over to her mother and asked, "Why is the bride dressed in white?"

"Because white represents happiness, and today is the happiest day of her life," her mother explained.

"Then why," the little girl asked, "is the groom dressed in black?"[4]

Let's make sure our husbands can look back on their wedding day as the happiest day in their lives. It can be if you and I recognize that our role as wives is to be a gift of God to our spouses—a crown, a blessing, and a prize to complement and fulfill them.

The Ultimate Picture

I want to close with the most beautiful portrait of marriage ever painted. I shiver with God-bumps when I think of the awesome illustration God gives us in his Word. He likens the special relationship between husband and wife to the loving relationship Christ has with his bride, the Church. Paul explains the analogy in Ephesians 5:31–33: "As the Scriptures say, 'A man leaves his father and mother and is joined to his wife, and the two are united into one.' This is a great mystery, but it is an illustration of the way Christ and the church are one. So again I say, each man must love his wife as he loves himself, and the wife must respect her husband" (NLT).

Marriage is God's design, not man's creation. It can and should be a beautiful reflection of Christ and the Church. The truth is, you have been created and designed to be your husband's loving counterpart—to complete an eternal picture that ultimately brings praise and glory to God. Relish the responsibility. Cherish your role. Choose today to be a positive wife!

POWER POINT

⚙ **Read:** Ephesians 3:14–19; Philippians 3:12–21. In his prayer for the early Christians in Ephesians 3, Paul reminds us of God's love and strength at work in our lives. How is Paul's prayer helpful to you personally as a wife? Paul talks about his high calling in Philippians 3:14 (KJV). How would you describe your high calling? Where is your true citizenship, and how does that affect your focus in life?

🕎 **Pray:** O marvelous Creator, thank you for the wonderful blessing of being a wife. Thank you for my husband. Thank you for the strengths and weaknesses we both bring into our marriage. Help us to complement, bless, and serve each other. Help me to be a crown and a joy to my husband, and keep me from being a detriment to him. Most importantly, keep my heart and mind focused on you. I want to live in the light of your love and allow it to overflow to those around me, especially my husband. In Jesus' name, amen.

💡 **Remember:** "For this reason a man will leave his father and mother and be united to his wife, and they will become one flesh" (Genesis 2:24).

☺ **Do:** Divide a piece of paper in half. On one side put your name, and on the other side put your husband's name. On your half, list some of your strengths and weaknesses. Across from those qualities, on your husband's half of the page, list the strengths and weaknesses he has that complement or help equalize yours. Notice how God has made you a good fit for one another.

It's Not about You!
It's about God's Power Working through You

I could not do without Thee, I cannot stand alone,
I have no strength or goodness, no wisdom of my own;
But Thou, beloved Savior, Art all in all to me!
And perfect strength in weakness is theirs who lean on Thee!

—F. R. Havergal

The other day my friend Rachel dropped off her daughter, Lane, to visit my daughter. As Lane entered our house she exclaimed, "It feels so good in here!" I didn't understand her statement until her mother walked through the door behind her, exhausted and dripping with sweat.

"There's something wrong with one of the belts in our car," Rachel explained, "and we had to drive over here with no power steering and no air conditioning."

Imagine driving with no air conditioning or power steering in the Texas summer heat! And if you have ever had the power steering go out in your car, you know how difficult it is to try to turn the steering wheel by your own power. It takes every bit of energy, strength, and muscle power you can muster. There is a marked difference between power steering and the lack thereof.

No one would choose to drive an automobile without power steering. Yet isn't it funny how often we try to maneuver and drive down the road of life in our own strength and power? We tend to want to depend on ourselves instead of depending on God's power at work in our lives.

21

The picture that comes to my mind is of Fred and Wilma Flintstone pedaling around Bedrock in their self-powered Stone Age car. It's only when we operate in the realm of God's direction and strength that we can enjoy the benefits of a power-driven ride.

I'm not saying we should sit back and assume no responsibility for where we're going or how we get there. As positive wives we must choose to live a godly life, but the good news is that we don't have to try to live it by our own power. The beauty of the Christian walk is that we have God's glorious power working in and through us. The apostle Paul put it this way in his letter to the Philippian Christians: "Therefore, my dear friends, as you have always obeyed—not only in my presence, but now much more in my absence—continue to work out your salvation with fear and trembling, for it is God who works in you to will and to act according to his good purpose" (Philippians 2:12–13). It's our choice to obey; it's God's work to carry out his purpose within us.

His Mighty Power in Us—Think of It!

Trevor Baskerville tells the story of his visit to a great hydro-electric plant. The guide took him out on the mile-long dam, and the two stood there watching the vast amount of water pouring over it.

"What percent of the power from this river do you actually transform into electricity, and how much goes over the dam and is lost?" Trevor asked the guide.

The guide shook his head and replied, "We don't use even a one-hundredth part of it."

Stunned, Trevor thought to himself, *How much of the power of God do I transform into usefulness, and how much is unused and lost?*[1]

Oh, to think of the power available to us—and yet we rarely recognize it, much less use it! Paul longed deeply for the early Christians to recognize God's great power at work in their lives. In Ephesians 1:18–20 we read, "I pray also that the eyes of your heart may be enlightened in order that you may know the hope to which he has called you, the riches of his glorious inheritance in the saints, and his incomparably great power for us who believe. That power is like the working of his mighty strength, which he exerted in Christ when he raised him from the dead and seated him at his right hand in the heavenly realms." Wow! Did I read that correctly? The same resurrection power that raised Christ from the dead is at work in us! Think of the magnitude of his resurrection power!

Later in his letter to the Ephesians, Paul continues, "Now to him who is able to do immeasurably more than all we ask or imagine, according to his power that is at work within us, to him be glory in the church and in Christ Jesus throughout all generations, for ever and ever!" (Ephesians 3:20–21). What do *you* need God's power and strength for? Is it patience? Understanding? Maybe it's having a kind tongue. Do you need help overcoming bitterness and anger? Are you having trouble forgiving? Or do you struggle with being an encourager?

Dear sister, there is hope, because the power of God's Spirit is at work in our lives. He is able to do more than we ask or imagine. God has given us the blessed opportunity to pray and ask for his help, strength, guidance, and power. James reminds us, "You do not have, because you do not ask God" (James 4:2). God's power is available for the asking. When is the last time you looked to God and asked him to work mightily in your life?

Remote and Release Control

Just a moment ago I picked up the remote control and pushed the button that reads Power to turn on the CD player in my stereo system. I love listening to soothing classical music as I write. It's easy to use that remote—to sit in the comfort of my own chair and press buttons to create the perfect work environment. I must admit, I enjoy the feeling of power and control that comes from having the remote in my hand. I'm almost as bad as my husband in front of the TV!

I think most of us would agree that we like the tempting, delicious feeling of being in control—and I'm talking about control over much bigger things than my stereo system. What do wives want to control? Circumstances, for one. We want to keep the people and things around us healthy, happy, and safe. Our families, for two. Many of us want to control our husbands and children—to micromanage their every word and action. Stop for a moment and ask yourself: What are some areas that you try to control?

We tend to think that if everything and everyone is under our control, then life will be free from worry or pain. Isn't that funny? How can we even begin to think that we can control things better than God? Do we really believe we're smarter than he is? Why do we think we can or should prevent every heartache from happening?

Certainly, in most situations, there is a time to take action. Giving control of our lives to God doesn't mean we let go of our responsibilities. It simply means that we leave the worry and the results to God.

Queen Esther found herself in a situation that was out of her control. You would think that, as queen, she could or would have been in control of almost everything in her life. But even she could not control the bleak outlook for the Jews (and for herself, for she was one of them) who were doomed by decree to be killed. Esther wisely and graciously acted on her responsibility to go before the king, but not before telling the people of Israel to pray and fast before God on her—and their— behalf. Esther recognized her responsibility, but she also relied on God's power. What a good model for wives to follow!

We may see flaws and weaknesses in our husbands and think it's our job to take control and change their ways. But that's not our job; it's God's. We do not have the power to turn our spouses' hearts or convict their minds or change their ways. That's God's work, and we can go to him in prayer—to ask God for his power and leadership in the situation. What is our job or responsibility? Our first responsibility is to pray for our husbands, asking God to do his mighty work in them in ways we can't imagine. There may be times when we need to lovingly suggest a change of course to our husbands or, as in Esther's case, wisely petition against a dangerous decision; but our first responsibility is to release the need to be in control to our wise and loving heavenly Father.

Recognizing Our Weaknesses

Classical Christian writer and thinker François Fénelon (1651–1715) said, "It is amazing how strong we become when we begin to understand what weaklings we are!"[2] Of course, "weakling" is not a popular label in today's survivor-mentality world. We are taught to value self-reliance and strength from an early age. Yet the Bible says that being an effective Christian involves recognizing that we are weak and God is strong. In a passage commonly referred to as the Beatitudes, Jesus says, "Blessed [happy] are the poor in spirit, for theirs is the kingdom of heaven" (Matthew 5:3).

"Poor in spirit" means being totally dependent on God. It means acknowledging that we are bankrupt in and of ourselves. We are powerless, but he is powerful. Fénelon went on to say, "Happy are they who throw themselves with bowed head and closed eyes into the arms of the Father of mercies and God of all consolation."[3]

How wonderful to know that our loving and capable God wants to pour his power through our weak little clay pots! Our lives may not be everything we wanted; our spouses may not be perfect; our living conditions may not be all we hoped for; we may be sorely disappointed

"Not by might nor by power, but by my Spirit," says the LORD Almighty. —Zechariah 4:6 ☺

with our own behavior. Yet despite our weaknesses, we can still look to a redeeming God to shine his light through us. Paul gave the Corinthian church these words of encouragement:

> For God, who said, "Let light shine out of darkness," made his light shine in our hearts to give us the light of the knowledge of the glory of God in the face of Christ.
>
> But we have this treasure in jars of clay to show that this all-surpassing power is from God and not from us. We are hard pressed on every side, but not crushed; perplexed, but not in despair; persecuted, but not abandoned; struck down, but not destroyed. We always carry around in our body the death of Jesus, so that the life of Jesus may also be revealed in our body. (2 Corinthians 4:6–10)

What is your greatest weakness or challenge in your marriage? We all know marriage is not a stroll down Easy Street; it's more like a bumpy drive down Human Flaws and Weaknesses Lane. Relationships are difficult because they are the bonding together of two limited, imperfect human beings. The question is not, "Do you have challenges?" The question is, "Where do you go for help, power, and strength through the challenges?" As positive wives, we need to recognize our weaknesses and look to God for our strength. In ourselves we are poor; in God we are wealthy. As Paul said later to the Corinthians, "For when I am weak [in human strength], then am I [truly] strong (able, powerful in divine strength)" (2 Corinthians 12:10 AMP).

Putting Power into Practice

It's one thing to talk about God's power at work in our lives; it's another to actually apply it. How do we get from the ethereal idea to the practical application? We can look to no better model than that of

Jesus as he was preparing to leave this earth. As he talked with his disciples, he told them how to put into practice all of the heavenly lessons they had learned from him.

After the Last Supper, Jesus began his journey to the Garden of Gethsemane. Along the way he stopped at a vineyard for a life lesson. We can read his discourse in John 15:1–5:

> I am the true vine, and my Father is the gardener. He cuts off every branch in me that bears no fruit, while every branch that does bear fruit he prunes so that it will be even more fruitful. You are already clean because of the word I have spoken to you. Remain in me, and I will remain in you. No branch can bear fruit by itself; it must remain in the vine. Neither can you bear fruit unless you remain in me.
>
> I am the vine; you are the branches. If a man remains in me and I in him, he will bear much fruit; apart from me you can do nothing.

We can glean a clear message from Jesus' words: If we try to be productive in bearing spiritual fruit on our own, we won't succeed; but if we remain in him and he remains in us, we will be effective and fruitful. Two questions jump out at me. First, what does it mean to be fruitful? For that answer we need to look at what the Bible means by the word *fruit.* In Paul's letter to the Galatians, he talks about the power of living by God's Spirit. He says that God's presence at work in us results in the fruit of the Spirit, and here's what that fruit looks like: "love, joy, peace, patience, kindness, goodness, faithfulness, gentleness and self-control" (Galatians 5:22–23). Now that's a beautiful list of qualities! Imagine if all wives exhibited those qualities in their homes and marriages. How lovely!

Does this fruit represent natural, human qualities? In other words, do we typically respond to difficult situations with patience and self-control? Are we generally joyful, gentle, and kind by nature? Do love and faithfulness naturally flow from our raw personalities? Not in our own power! I may just be speaking for myself here, but I have a feeling you also struggle with producing this fruit in your own strength. Thank goodness bearing fruit is a "God thing" and not a "me thing"! We don't have to try to produce fruit. God's Holy Spirit accomplishes this work in us and through us.

Jesus says that we cannot produce fruit on our own; rather, the key to being fruitful is to "remain in him." Which leads me to my second question: What does it mean to remain in him? Take a look at the Amplified Bible's version of John 15:4: "Dwell in Me, and I will dwell in you. [Live in Me, and I will live in you.] Just as no branch can bear fruit of itself without abiding in (being vitally united to) the vine, neither can you bear fruit unless you abide in Me."

To dwell, live, and abide with someone denotes a strong, active relationship with that person. Remaining in Christ doesn't refer to a casual visit with Jesus now and then (say, on holidays or occasional Sunday mornings). Rather, it indicates a depth of closeness with him that's lived moment by moment throughout each day. When we remain, dwell, and abide in Christ, we experience the daily joy of a vibrant, powerful, life-giving relationship with him.

Brother Lawrence, a seventeenth century monk who worked in the kitchen at the Discalced Carmelite Order in Paris, is someone who abided with Christ—he called it "practicing God's presence"—every moment of every day. He took great joy in the mundane tasks of his kitchen work, seeing himself as "a servant of the servants of God." He not only developed a strong prayer life through the time he set aside for prayer every day, he also walked and talked with God all day long. Remembering that Brother Lawrence never received a formal education, read his words of profound insight as a testimony of what God can do in the life of a willing vessel: "As for my set hours of prayer, they are only a continuation of the same exercise. Sometimes I imagine myself as a stone before a sculptor from which he will carve a beautiful statue. Presenting myself before God, I ask him to form his perfect image in my soul and make me entirely like himself."[4]

If only we had such passion for God in our daily lives as wives! But what does it mean to "practice God's presence" all day long? It means continually turning our hearts and minds toward God and his truth. Whether the circumstances of our days are mundane and unpleasant or joyful and glorious, we choose to turn our eyes heavenward. Challenges and struggles take on a different air when we see them in light of eternity. The Sculptor's sharp chisel may be just the thing that fashions us into a beautiful work of art.

I'm reminded of Colossians 3:1–2: "Since, then, you have been raised with Christ, set your hearts on things above, where Christ is seated at the right hand of God. Set your minds on things above, not on earthly things." When we set our minds on "things above," we begin to have a more eternal perspective. Standing behind an annoying person in the checkout line becomes an opportunity to pray for someone who's hurting. Feeling frustrated with our husbands becomes an opportunity to ask God to work in their lives and in ours, conforming us to be the people we ought to be for God's glory.

She Knows

Edith Schaeffer was a positive wife who lived and served others in God's power and strength, even though her circumstances were less than perfect. Deeply concerned about the spiritual state of the European churches and pastors after World War II, Edith and her husband, Francis, became missionaries in Europe. They wondered what possible impact one simple family could have on an entire continent of people who were discouraged and exhausted from the ravages of war. But their hearts' desire was to inspire the Europeans to faith and challenge them to battle for the truth of God's Word.

The Schaeffers' first years as missionaries were not easy. Edith and the children lived in small, shabby apartments while Francis traveled to different areas of Europe to speak and teach. At times the Schaeffer family lived as nomads, traveling tirelessly across the continent to start Bible studies and camps for boys and girls. They also wrote a Bible study curriculum and sent their materials all over Europe.

Although they were quite busy, the Schaeffers were always open to opportunities to share God's truth with the people around them, whether students, villagers, or soldiers. Their warmth and hospitality began to draw more people to them to ask questions about Christianity.

In 1955 the Schaeffers faced a big challenge when it became necessary for them to leave their home in Switzerland and find another place to live. The timing couldn't have been worse. Their son Franky had come down with polio and was severely paralyzed, and their daughter Susan had rheumatic fever. Both children eventually recovered from their illnesses, but at that point the family was in a terrible bind.

They had a very limited time to find their next home, not to mention limited resources to pay for it. But after many disappointments and setbacks in the house search, Edith finally found a place she believed was God's answer to their needs. There was only one problem: The down payment was one thousand dollars. The Schaeffers didn't have the money, but they knew God could provide it if he wanted them to move into this home.

So, trusting in God's wisdom and provision, Edith prayed that if God wanted them to have the house, he would send them the exact amount they needed by the exact time they needed it. And amazingly, on the day the down payment was required, a letter arrived containing a check for one thousand dollars!

Not long after the Schaeffers moved into their God-given house, their daughter Priscilla called and asked if she could bring a wealthy college classmate home for the weekend. At first Edith was tempted to decline. Their new chalet was far from ready for company. But when Priscilla told her that the classmate had been studying different religions and didn't know what to believe, Edith agreed the girl should come for a visit. She welcomed Priscilla's friend warmly and gently explained God's truth to her.

This event marked a turning point in the Schaeffers' ministry. Soon the word was out that the Schaeffers would welcome anyone into their home and answer honest questions about God. They named their chalet "L'Abri," which means "the shelter" in French. It soon became an international study center, where people from all over the world came to learn and discuss the truth about God. Edith and Francis lovingly shared their home and their faith. Proving they were right was never as important as treating their guests in a loving way. Branches of L'Abri were eventually opened in a number of other countries. Francis died in 1984, but Edith continued to work with L'Abri. Her life remains a testimony of the power of God, poured out through one positive wife who trusted in his strength and not her own.[5]

Sacred Covenant

"A good marriage is not a contract between two persons but a sacred covenant between three," writes author Donald Kaufman.[6] How true! Making God a vital part of marriage adds a powerful dimension of strength to its foundation. As Ecclesiastes 4:12 says, "A cord of three strands is not quickly broken." Of course, it would be lovely if all of our husbands relied on God's strength. But whether they do or not, we have a responsibility to do so. I learned long ago that I couldn't force or create a strong spiritual walk for my husband, Curt. He is solely responsible for his own relationship with God. The same is true for your husband. But as wives we can choose to rely on God for ourselves and invite God's power to be at work in our marriages.

Proverbs 19:14 tells us, "House and riches are the inheritance from fathers, but a wise, understanding, *and* prudent wife is from the Lord" (AMP). Oh, what a gift from God we can be to our husbands if only we choose to rely on God's power and reflect the fruit of his Spirit in our homes! The lovely qualities of a positive wife are not something we produce through our own meager efforts; they are the evidence of God at work in our lives. Our part is to practice his presence and dwell in his love moment by moment, day by day. As we do, our lives and our marriages will be strengthened with the peace, hope, and joy that comes from dwelling and abiding in him.

POWER POINT

⚙ **Read:** Romans 8. What encouragement do you receive from these words of Paul? Identify several verses that remind you of God's power and strength at work in your life.

♡ **Pray:** Wonderful, powerful, heavenly Father, thank you for working mightily in my life. I praise you for your Son, who died and rose again on our behalf. I praise you for your Holy Spirit, whom you give to all who believe. Thank you for the power and strength your Spirit gives me day by day. Help me to dwell in you moment by moment. Produce the beautiful fruit of love, joy, peace, patience, kindness, goodness, faithfulness, gentleness, and self-control in me. May your power work through my weaknesses and make a positive impact on my marriage, my home, and my community. In Jesus' name, amen.

💡 **Remember:** "My grace is sufficient for you, for my power is made perfect in weakness" (2 Corinthians 12:9).

☺ **Do:** Designate a day this week that you will devote to dwelling in God's presence all day long, even as you go about your normal routine at work and/or at home. You may find it helpful to make it a day of fasting (from food or sweets or soft drinks) as a way of reminding yourself to walk continuously in his presence all day long.

Power Principle #1

THe Power OF Love

Love is a friendship that has caught fire. It is quiet understanding, mutual confidence, sharing, and forgiving. It is a loyalty through good and bad. It settles for less than perfection and makes allowances for human weaknesses.

—Ann Landers

This is my prayer: that your love may abound more and more in knowledge and depth of insight.

—Philippians 1:9

The Truth about True Love
Dispelling the Deadly Marriage Myths

The true measure of loving...is to love without measure.

—St. Bernard of Clairvaux

Marilou and Hank had been married for seventeen years. (Like many people in this book, their names have been changed to protect their identities.) They had experienced a few bumps along the way, but overall their marriage was a good one. They enjoyed their upscale life together, traveling, raising kids, working, and volunteering for several charities. Typically, Hank worked many extra hours at the office during the week so he could spend most of the weekend at home with his family. Marilou spent much of her free time on the weekdays playing tennis at the club.

Sounds pretty good, doesn't it? Unfortunately, there was one big problem: Marilou had a *mumpsimus*.

Now you're probably thinking that Marilou had some kind of incurable disease. Let me reassure you, a mumpsimus is completely curable. According to my dad, the definition of *mumpsimus* is "a persistent belief in a mistaken idea." Mumpsimuses have been around for years. You probably have a few yourself. Here are some common ones:

- Sticks and stones will break my bones, but words will never hurt me.

- Love means never having to say you're sorry.

- Blondes are not as intelligent as brunettes.

What was Marilou's mumpsimus? She believed that being "in love" was something every person deserves—that the state of being "in love" was more important than a marriage commitment. So after seventeen years of marriage, Marilou left Hank for the tennis pro at the club. She told him, "I love you, but I'm not *in love* with you anymore." Because of her mumpsimus, Marilou threw away seventeen years of memories, dreams, and family ties for the ever-fleeting sensation of being "in love."

It's amazing how many mistaken beliefs exist concerning love and marriage. This chapter is devoted to dispelling some of the myths that can creep into our thinking about love and lifelong commitment. As you will see, these myths have been destroying marriages throughout the ages. But as Jesus said, "You will know the truth, and the truth will set you free" (John 8:32). Knowing and applying the truth about love can strengthen your relationship with your husband and enrich your marriage.

Let's examine three of the most common marriage myths and shine the light of truth on them.

Myth #1

There is one "true love" out there for me.
I must find him, marry him, and live happily ever after.

Hollywood movies, love songs, and romance novels have done a number on us by creating a surreal picture of the perfect romance. The idea that there is only one true love out there for each person is dangerous in marriage.

Let's say that several months (or maybe even days) after the honeymoon, reality sets in, and you begin to discover some of your spouse's glaring weaknesses. *Uh-oh,* you say to yourself, *he's not as perfect as I thought he was.* (The truth is, he is probably coming to that same conclusion about you!) If you hold to the mind-set that each of us has one true love out there, what do you do when you realize that your spouse is not so lovable at times? It's easy to begin doubting your marriage and thinking, *Maybe I made a mistake. Maybe this person is not the one for me.* See the danger? You may even be tempted to go on the prowl outside your marriage for that one special soul mate, telling yourself, *If I've made a mistake, that means Mr. Right must still be out there.*

When we subscribe to the notion that there is one perfect person for each of us, we tend to believe that once we find him, there will be no work involved in the relationship. Certainly, we should look for a spouse who exhibits the character qualities and Christian values that we know we want in a lifelong partner. But when we find that seemingly perfect guy, we must accept the fact that love will still be work. True love doesn't mean having a relationship of ease; it means making the continual choice to love and forgive.

In fact, one of the most important truths we can grasp about true love is that it isn't discovered; it's created. True love is the result of choosing to love your spouse every day. It sprouts and grows through the process of making that daily choice. Many couples who have been happily married for more than thirty years have told me that their love is much deeper and truer now than it was when they first married. The love they experienced in their early years is only a small fraction of the fullness of love they currently feel for each other. Their true love was created—not simply discovered.

My dad has said to me many times, "Karol, make a decision, and then make it a right decision." On my wedding day, I made a decision and a vow to commit my life to my husband, Curt. Now my job is to continually work to make that decision a right one through my loving actions toward him.

Choosing to love is not always easy, but that's what we're commanded to do as Christians. Jesus didn't tell us, "Love those who are easy to love, and when it gets difficult, give up." On the contrary, his message to us is to love one another, even if it isn't easy. He said in Luke 6:31–36:

> Do to others as you would have them do to you. If you love those who love you, what credit is that to you? Even "sinners" love those who love them. And if you do good to those who are good to you, what credit is that to you? Even "sinners" do that. And if you lend to those from whom you expect repayment, what credit is that to you? Even "sinners" lend to "sinners", expecting to be repaid in full. But love your enemies, do good to them, and lend to them without expecting to get anything back. Then your reward will be great, and you will be sons of the Most High, because he is kind to the ungrateful and wicked. Be merciful, just as your Father is merciful.

As Christians, we are called to a higher kind of love. We must love not only those who are easy to love—anyone can do that!—but also those who are unlovely or difficult. This is especially important in marriage. We must continue to love our husbands beyond the occasional ugliness and the inevitable challenges we come up against. Married love requires a kind of *grueling devotion*. We must be devoted enough and committed enough to be willing to crawl through the mire and muck of life, loving not only the lovable things about our husbands but the unlovable things too.

Certainly, this is the way God loves us: beyond our ugliness and sin. Through our difficulties. In spite of our faults. And this is the kind of love he desires for us to pour out to others, beginning with our spouses.

Myth #2

In order to love others, I must first love myself.

This myth was actually born from a truth (as is often the case with myths). Many well-meaning people have taken the words of Jesus found in Matthew 22:39, "Love your neighbor as yourself," and confused them to mean that we must love ourselves first before we can love others. Oops! The truth went right over their heads! In this passage Jesus is making the basic assumption that we already have a self-centered tendency to take care of ourselves, to look out for number one. His command is for us to love others in the same way—to take care of them and look out for them with the same kind of interest and attentiveness.

Nowhere in the Bible are we told to focus on loving ourselves. You may be thinking, *No problem. I don't even like myself, much less love myself!* Many of us struggle with a poor self-concept. If you think about it, we're all pretty sinful and yucky people at times, aren't we? It's understandable for us to be frustrated with ourselves, especially when we see our own glaring flaws and weaknesses.

But God doesn't want us to be down on ourselves. After all, he's not down on us! God values us so highly that he sent his only Son to pay for our sins on the cross. We are so significant to our heavenly Father that he has invited us to spend eternity with him.

For the sake of your marriage, it's vitally important that you recognize your eternal worth and value. Why? If you don't recognize your

A new command I give you: Love one another. As I have loved you, so you must love one another. —John 13:34

41

personal value in Christ, you will tend to look to your spouse for your value—even demand it. But depending on your husband to make you feel good about yourself will only lead to fear, disappointment, and unmet needs.

Can I let you in on a little secret? I have struggled with my own self-concept for many years and have tried at times to place the burden on Curt to make me feel better about myself. The truth is, my self-esteem must come from above and not from my spouse (or anyone else for that matter). Here are four keys that have helped me to develop a strong sense of my personal worth in Christ. I think you will find them helpful too.

1. Stop thinking about yourself.

Being constantly down on yourself is a sign that you're thinking and focusing your mind on yourself. If I dwell, dwell, dwell on "me, myself, and I," most likely I will be disappointed with what I see! Our focus can consume us, so let's be thoughtful about what we concentrate on. Read the following verses to see where we truly ought to direct our thoughts.

> Hebrews 12:2: Let us fix our eyes on Jesus, the author and perfecter of our faith, who for the joy set before him endured the cross, scorning its shame, and sat down at the right hand of the throne of God.

> Philippians 2:4–7: Don't think only about your own affairs, but be interested in others, too, and what they are doing. Your attitude should be the same that Christ Jesus had. Though he was God, he did not demand and cling to his rights as God. He made himself nothing; he took the humble position of a slave and appeared in human form. (NLT)

Colossians 3:2: Set your minds on things above, not on earthly things.

Isaiah 26:3: You will keep him in perfect peace, whose mind is stayed on You, because he trusts in You. (NKJV)

As we turn our focus toward the wonder of God, the sacrifice of Jesus, and the needs and interests of others, our own inadequacies become less important to us. Which leads me to the next point:

2. Pour yourself into loving, serving, and forgiving others.

Nothing will give your self-concept a boost more than a healthy dose of loving others. As you actively and honestly love the people around you, you are strengthened because you know you have done something good for someone else.

Jesus said, "Give, and it will be given to you. A good measure, pressed down, shaken together and running over, will be poured into your lap. For with the measure you use, it will be measured to you" (Luke 6:38). Are you generous with love? It will return to you in the same portion. In giving, we receive.

3. Consider your lifestyle.

Often we feel bad about ourselves because we are living in some degree of disobedience to God and his commands. Abundant joy is possible only as we live our lives in obedience to him. Listen to Jesus' words to his disciples in John 15:10–12: "If you obey my commands, you will remain in my love, just as I have obeyed my Father's commands and remain in his love. I have told you this so that my joy may be in you and that your joy may be complete. My command is this: Love each other as I have loved you."

Oh, what joy we experience when we walk in God's ways, follow his life principles, and obey his commands! What pain, sorrow, and heartache we feel when we live in rebellion against him! Living a sinful lifestyle may feel good for a time, but it eventually takes a toll on our self-esteem. Take a moment to examine your life. Is there a habitual sin you need to turn from? Certainly as Christians we stand forgiven in God's grace, but the consequences of sin can still cause great pain in our lives and in the lives of others.

4. Recognize that God created you, loves you, and is still working on you.

You and I are beloved works in progress. Psalm 139:13–14 reminds us that our heavenly Father created us and skillfully fashioned us in our mother's womb. We are wonderfully made by God! Our strengths and weaknesses are all a part of the wonderful package he put together. Is he done with us? Is he still working on us? Consider the following verses:

> In him we were also chosen, having been predestined according to the plan of him who works out everything in conformity with the purpose of his will, in order that we, who were the first to hope in Christ, might be for the praise of his glory. (Ephesians 1:11–12)

> For we are God's workmanship, created in Christ Jesus to do good works, which God prepared in advance for us to do. (Ephesians 2:10)

> He who began a good work in you will carry it on to completion until the day of Christ Jesus. (Philippians 1:6)

> How great is the love the Father has lavished on us, that we should be called children of God! And that is what we are! (1 John 3:1)

What could be more confidence building than knowing that God, the Creator of the universe, designed you, loves you, forgives you, and is still working on you? May we draw encouragement and strength from this truth! God isn't looking down on us and shaking his head back and forth, saying, "Will they ever get it right?" No, God is looking lovingly at us through eyes of grace, saying, "I love you, and I am for you." Feel his warm embrace! His loving arms are always there to hold you through sorrow, help you through challenges, and head you in a positive direction down the path he has planned for you.

Myth #3

I can fall out of love with my spouse.

Remember the story of Hank and Marilou at the beginning of the chapter? The idea that marital love is something we can fall in and out of is an unfortunate, yet common, belief. It's almost humorous to think of people strolling merrily down the path of life, falling in love, vowing to stay in love forever, but then somehow magically falling out of it. It's as if they're on autopilot and they have to go wherever love takes them. They have no power or say-so in the matter. When love is defined as a feeling that comes and goes, it takes on a mind of its own.

Well, these myths may work well in the movies, but they won't float the marriage boat. As positive wives, we need to make sure our definition of love is grounded and sure.

In his book *The Four Loves,* C. S. Lewis describes the different types of love we experience in life. He begins with the "humblest and most widely diffused of loves," *affection* (called *storge* by the Greeks). The beauty of this love is seen, for example, in the relationship between a mother and child. Affection is a kind of love in and of itself, but it also enters into other loves and enhances them.

According to Lewis, the second type of love is *friendship* (*philia* in the Greek, which is where we get the word *Philadelphia,* the "City of Brotherly Love"). These days most people don't put friendship in the

☺

category of "love," but Aristotle classified *philia* among the great virtues. As Lewis explains, "To the Ancients, friendship seemed the happiest and most fully human of all loves; the crown of life and the school of virtue. The modern world, in comparison, ignores it." Friendship is a valid form of love. It expresses the beauty of companionship. It is more a choice than a natural affection.

The next love Lewis presents to his readers is *eros*. This is what we generally recognize as being "in love." It is the love between lovers. *Eros* is a deep, all-encompassing desire for the beloved, and sexual pleasure is one of the ways this type of love is expressed.

The last love Lewis describes is *charity*, or divine love (*agape* in the Greek). This is a love that transcends all earthly loves. It is a selfless love, a gift-love, the kind modeled by God in his abundant and forgiving love for us. We see *agape* love eloquently described in 1 Corinthians 13:4–8. You will recognize this passage as one that is often read at weddings: "Love is patient, love is kind. It does not envy, it does not boast, it is not proud. It is not rude, it is not self-seeking, it is not easily angered, it keeps no record of wrongs. Love does not delight in evil but rejoices with the truth. It always protects, always trusts, always hopes, always perseveres. Love never fails."[1]

Does that sound like a description of something we can fall in and out of on a whim? I don't think so! First Corinthians 13 describes a profound love, a love that involves the giving of ourselves fully to another person.

Typically when people say they have "fallen out of love," what they really mean is, "I am no longer willing to work at loving you. I would rather follow my own pleasures and look for someone else to make me feel good about myself." The kick of it all is that no one is easy to love. Granted, some people are easier to get along with than others; but all humans have their flaws. True love loves past the weaknesses and builds on the strengths. Love "bears all things, believes all things, hopes all things, endures all things," as the Bible says in 1 Corinthians 13:7 (NASB).

Which of the loves described by Lewis do we find in marriage? All four. Marriage encompasses natural affection, companionship, pleasure, and divine love. But how do we love like that? Are you as exasperated as I am when you read the description of love in 1 Corinthians 13? Take hope, dear sister! When it comes to love, we have divine help.

The Power to Love

Have you ever heard of a creature called *cryptobiotic tardigrade*? This strange little being can live for a hundred years in a deathlike state, withdrawn it its spiny shell. It can exist without water, oxygen, or heat; yet when it is moistened, it immediately springs back to life. Its legs and head poke out from its coffinlike shell. Amazing! The cryptobiotic tardigrade goes from a dormant state to vibrant life with just a touch of water.[2]

Sometimes we may feel as if our love for our husbands is in a dormant state, deadlike, if you will. What can resurrect that love? What can make and keep our love vibrant and strong? A little living water! The power and ability to love can be found at the fountain of true love, God himself. Read with me what I consider to be the most glorious and powerful love passage in the Bible:

> Dear friends, let us love one another, for love comes from God. Everyone who loves has been born of God and knows God. Whoever does not love does not know God, because God is love. This is how God showed his love among us: He sent his one and only Son into the world that we might live through him. This is love: not that we loved God, but that he loved us and sent his Son as an atoning sacrifice for our sins. Dear friends, since God so loved us, we also ought to love one another. No one has ever seen God;

but if we love one another, God lives in us and his love is made complete in us.

We know that we live in him and he in us, because he has given us of his Spirit. And we have seen and testify that the Father has sent his Son to be the Savior of the world. If anyone acknowledges that Jesus is the Son of God, God lives in him and he in God. And so we know and rely on the love God has for us.

God is love. Whoever lives in love lives in God, and God in him. In this way, love is made complete among us. (1 John 4:7–17)

To put it simply, love is a God-thing. Oh, what awesome and overwhelming love our heavenly Father has for us! Relish it. Enjoy it. Fill your heart with it! As we recognize and receive God's love for us, it awakens our love for those around us. Let us draw near to the source of this pure and beautiful love and drink from its fountain each and every day.

A Foundation of Truth

As we have reflected on the myths about love and marriage, have you recognized any mumpsimuses in your own relationship with your husband? Let's not end with a focus on myths; instead let's recap the chapter with the important truths we have gleaned from this study:

- *True love principle #1:* True love is not simply discovered; it is created, and it takes work.

- *True love principle #2:* Fully loving my spouse is not based on my own self-love, but more importantly in understanding my value from God's perspective.

- *True love principle #3:* Marital love is a commitment encompassing affection, friendship, pleasure, and selfless love.

By embracing these principles of true love, we can begin to build our marriages on a sure foundation. A house of cards easily falls, but a house built on truth and love will stand through the tests of time and the winds of circumstance. As positive wives, let's not build our houses on myths but on the rock-solid truth of God's love.

POWER POINT

⚙ **Read:** Romans 8:28–39. What do you learn about God's love for us in this passage? Because we are genuinely loved, we are able to freely give love. How does this passage help you love your spouse in the truest sense of the word?

♡ **Pray:** God of love, Father of mercy, pour your beautiful and abundant love through me. I praise you because your love is perfectly fulfilling. Thank you for loving me so completely and purely. May I love my husband with this type of love. Give me the power and strength to love him with patience and kindness. Help me to bear all things, believe all things, and hope all things when it comes to our marriage commitment. Please allow me to be a reflection of your love in my home. In Christ's name, amen.

♀ **Remember:** "Dear friends, let us love one another, for love comes from God" (1 John 4:7).

☺ **Do:** Schedule an evening or Saturday-morning walk with your husband. While you're walking, tell him you have been reading a chapter in this book about the definition of love. Talk together about how our culture defines love and identify some of the misconceptions that exist; then discuss how you as a couple would define love. Finally, talk about how you can better show that love to each other.

4

The Truest Joy and the Toughest Journey

Filling Your Home with Forgiveness

The truest joys they seldom prove, Who free from quarrels live;
'Tis the most tender part of love, Each other to forgive.

—John Sheffield, Duke of Buckingham

July 1, 1992, was a life-changing day for Martha Edwards and her three young boys. Martha's husband, John, a Baylor Law School graduate and lawyer for the prestigious law firm Haynes and Boone, was working on a case at the Tarrant County Courthouse in nearby Fort Worth that particular day. A man named George Douglas Lott was also in the courthouse, facing sexual abuse charges. It is impossible to know exactly what was going through Lott's mind, but at 9:30 A.M. he pulled out a gun and opened fire inside the courtroom. John Edwards was standing in the courtroom when the shots were fired. He ran to get help, but Lott followed him and shot him at point-blank range in the courthouse stairwell. John died, having heroically drawn the assailant from his targets in the courtroom and saving many more lives that fateful day. As for Lott, he was eventually captured when he entered a television station asking for an interview with the lead newscaster.

Martha Edwards was also a hero in this story. A strong Christian woman, Martha chose to respond to her loss with forgiveness rather than bitterness. Ten years after the event, she was quoted in the *Dallas*

Morning News saying, "I had to learn how to forgive and how to move forward and to learn how powerful forgiveness is." She added that with the help of her family, friends, and faith, she had put away hatred and contempt long ago.

"They say you either become bitter or better, and that's so true," she said. "We appreciate and respect the past. That's part of the legacy. But we truly lead a wonderful, fun, and balanced life, and the boys truly have benefited from a positive outlook." Martha gave her children and herself one of the greatest gifts a person can give: the gift of forgiveness. She did this not so much for George Lott's benefit, although he may have taken some comfort in knowing that her family's anger no longer raged against him; but rather for the benefit of all who knew and loved John. There is tremendous healing power in the choice to forgive and move on.[1]

As difficult as it is to forgive a total stranger, as Martha did, it can be even more difficult to forgive a person we know and love—a husband, for example. But forgiveness is like a beautiful aroma that fills our homes with the fragrance of true love. Bitterness and anger have a smell, too, but it's the putrid stench of decay and destruction. Unforgiveness destroys a home; forgiveness builds it up. Since marriage is comprised of two sinful people working together under one roof, we need to make sure we have the heavenly scent of forgiveness continually permeating the atmosphere. I like what Martin Luther said: "A happy marriage is the union of two good forgivers."[2]

Faces of Forgiveness

Isn't it odd how many of the traits that first were so endearing in our husbands turn out to be just the ones that become offensive to us? Take, for instance, Mark's passion for taking Susan out on the town to expensive restaurants and spending lavishly on her while they were dating.

As a college girl, she was swept off her feet by his royal treatment. Now Mark's spendaholic tendencies make her angry and frustrated every time she sits down to balance the family checkbook.

Or consider Steve's humble spirit and gentle personality that Lori so admired while they were courting. Over the years this same trait has made her angry and resentful; Steve's lack of aggressiveness in business situations has caused him to be bypassed for promotions, and the family income has been impacted. Steve's once-valued trait has become a giant, ugly monster living in their home.

Let's face it. All of us get angry with our husbands. Some of us just do it more frequently than others. In marriage, we must continually forgive our spouses for:

- Intentional offenses—things that are said or done to purposely hurt us

- Unintentional mistakes—accidents that affect us in some way

- Faults and weaknesses—idiosyncrasies that bug us or let us down (of course, we have very few, if any, of these ourselves!)

- Past hurts—old wounds that our memories keep dragging up (often distorted to seem worse than they really were at the time)

- Assumptions—thoughts we have about our spouses' motives or intentions that cause us to feel angry or hurt (what great mind readers we are!)

Whatever the offense, we will have a hard time forgiving our husbands if we don't have a clear understanding of what forgiveness is. How would you define forgiveness? Webster defines the verb *forgive* this way: "to give up resentment against or the desire to punish; stop being angry with; pardon—to give up all claim to punish." In other words, although we may feel we have the right to be angry or hold resentment, we lay down that right and choose to forgive instead.

But forgiveness is more than an act of the will; it's an attitude of the heart. It's not just a one-time event; it's a continual act. Matthew 18:21–22 records a discussion between Peter and Jesus that underlines the continual nature of forgiveness. "Then Peter came up to Him and said, Lord, how many times may my brother sin against me, and I forgive him *and* let it go? [As many as] up to seven times? Jesus answered him, I tell you, not up to seven times, but seventy times seven!" (AMP).

In marriage, husbands and wives must stay in a mode of continual forgiveness. We must choose with our minds to forgive every time an old offense comes back to haunt us. (Come on, admit it—as women we tend to nurse old emotional wounds and replay them over and over again.) When we say, "I forgive you," we must forgive and keep forgiving, not nurse and rehearse the same old hurt a hundred times.

Sometimes a spouse makes repeated mistakes. My friend Holly, who is in her first year of marriage, has damaged or wrecked her hubby's car four times. Yes, count them, four—and the year is not over yet. What has Holly needed from Mac at least four times? Forgiveness! Thankfully, Mac has practiced the Matthew 18:22–23 principle beautifully and lovingly, fully forgiving his new wife for each mishap. (Of course, he *is* a little more cautious now about letting Holly drive his car.)

Does continual forgiveness mean that we give a spouse carte blanche to continue to cause hurt? Not at all! Remember our definition? Forgiveness is an act of the will and an attitude of the heart. It's a choice we make not to hold resentment toward the offender. It is a release of our right to be angry. It is not naiveté, stupidity, or a continual placement of ourselves in the pathway of danger or abuse. It is not the acceptance of another's sin. Even when Jesus forgave the woman accused of adultery, he told her, "Go and sin no more" (John 8:11 KJV). And the truth is, even though we may forgive an offense in our hearts and minds, certain responsibilities remain and certain consequences are unavoidable. (We will address these more deeply later in this chapter.)

Why Forgive?

John Plummer, a minister in Purcellville, Virginia, was haunted for many years by a Pulitzer Prize–winning photograph from the Vietnam War era. You may remember the picture yourself: a little Vietnamese girl, nine-year-old Phan Thi Kim Phuc, running down the road naked and horribly burned following a napalm attack of her village. For John this photo had deep significance. In 1972 he had been responsible for setting up the air strike on that village, called Trang Bang. He had been assured two times that there were no civilians in the area. And although he knew in his heart that he had done what he could to make sure there were no civilians in Trang Bang, he still felt a deep pain every time he saw the girl's picture. His information had been tragically wrong. He longed to tell her how sorry he was.

John became a Christian in 1990 and felt called into the ministry. Remarkably, in the summer of 1996, he learned that Kim Phuc was still alive and living in Toronto. The very next month, while attending a military reunion, he met someone who knew both the girl and the photographer. He also learned more of the story of that fateful day in 1972. Apparently Kim Phuc and her family had been taking refuge in a pagoda when a bomb fell on the building. Kim Phuc and others ran into the street, where they were hit with napalm dropped by another plane. As she fled, Kim Phuc ripped away her burning clothes. Two of her cousins died in the attack. The photographer, along with other journalists, poured water from their canteens on her burns. Just minutes after the famous photo was taken, she collapsed and was rushed to a hospital. She was operated on by a San Francisco plastic surgeon and spent fourteen months in hospitals.

Clothe yourselves with compassion, kindness, humility, gentleness and patience. —Colossians 3:12

John found out that Kim Phuc was going to speak at the Vietnam Veterans Memorial in Washington, D.C., so he went to hear her. During her address she said that if she ever had the opportunity to meet the pilot of the plane that was responsible for her injuries, she would tell him that she had forgiven him. She said that although they could not change what happened in the past, she hoped they could work together in the future.

Plummer managed to get word to her that he was in the audience and wanted to meet her. As the two stood face-to-face, Kim Phuc saw the depth of his grief, sorrow, and pain. She held out her arms to John and embraced him. As he repeated over and over again, "I'm sorry," she responded over and over again, "It's all right; it's all right. I forgive; I forgive." Plummer soon learned that Kim Phuc, although raised a Buddhist, had become a Christian in 1992.[3]

What would compel a young woman who'd been so emotionally scarred and physically wounded to forgive the person who caused it all? Although I do not know the details of Kim Phuc's journey toward forgiveness, I do know that the essence of Christian faith is rooted in forgiveness and love. Our heavenly Father poured out his forgiveness and love through Jesus. What happened to Kim Phuc was a terrible atrocity. The miracle is that she is filled today with love and forgiveness. With God all things are possible!

Why forgive? I believe there are three reasons.

1. We forgive because we are forgiven.

I am overcome with gratitude and love when I consider the forgiveness God pours out on us. If only we could grasp the magnitude of his abundant love described in Psalm 103! Relish with me the psalmist's words:

He made known his ways to Moses, his deeds to the people of Israel: The Lord is compassionate and gracious, slow to anger, abounding in love. He will not always accuse, nor will he harbor his anger forever; he does not treat us as our sins deserve or repay us according to our iniquities. For as high as the heavens are above the earth, so great is his love for those who fear him; as far as the east is from the west, so far has he removed our transgressions from us. As a father has compassion on his children, so the Lord has compassion on those who fear him; for he knows how we are formed, he remembers that we are dust. (Psalm 103:7–14)

Each of us has been forgiven of so much! What right do we have to deny forgiveness to one another? In Matthew 18 Jesus tells a parable about an unforgiving servant that speaks volumes about our obligation to forgive. A king wanted to settle accounts with his servants, so a man who owed him ten thousand talents (quite a large amount of money) was brought before the throne. The king ordered that the man, his family, and his possessions be sold in order to pay the debt, but the man begged and pleaded for mercy. The king took pity on him, cancelled the debt, and let him go.

That same man went straight to another servant who owed him a small amount of money and demanded payment. The debtor pleaded for mercy, but when he couldn't produce the money, the man had him thrown in jail. Several other servants saw what happened and reported the incident back to the king, who called the forgiven man back into the throne room.

"'You wicked servant,' he said, 'I canceled all that debt of yours because you begged me to. Shouldn't you have had mercy on your fellow servant just as I had on you?'" (Matthew 18:32–33). Then he turned the servant over to the jailers to be tortured until he could pay back everything he owed.

Forgiveness is our obligation. We have been forgiven; therefore, we must forgive others—especially our husbands! Ephesians 4:32 says it all: "Be kind and compassionate to one another, forgiving each other, just as in Christ God forgave you." Our obligation to forgive is so vital that Jesus gave the following admonition in his Sermon on the Mount: "For if you forgive men when they sin against you, your heavenly Father will also forgive you. But if you do not forgive men their sins, your Father will not forgive your sins" (Matthew 6:14–15).

Whoa! That's a strong statement. But let's be clear: God's forgiveness is not a direct result of our forgiveness. Rather, our failure to forgive others shows God that we either haven't recognized or don't appreciate the depth of his forgiveness toward us.

2. We forgive because it is emotionally healing.

As both Martha Edwards and Kim Phuc discovered, tremendous healing of the heart takes place when we extend forgiveness. When we fail to forgive, we're the ones who carry the burden—not the offender. Each time we refuse to forgive, we add heavy baggage to our hearts and minds.

Imagine that you come into marriage wearing a big, beautiful, empty backpack. Every time you refuse to forgive your spouse for an offense or fault, you pick up a five-pound bag of flour and put it in the backpack. Before long you are weighted down with a very heavy, back-breaking load, and that's not healthy—for you or your marriage.

Bitterness and anger keep us living in the past, causing us to become stagnant in our journey down the road of life. Forgiveness and love, on the other hand, allow us to live in the present and move forward into lives of productivity and victory. I think about Hebrews 12:1: "Therefore, since we are surrounded by such a great cloud of witnesses, let us throw off everything that hinders and the sin that so easily entangles, and let us run with perseverance the race marked out for us." Long-distance runners know they can't compete if they are wearing extra baggage, so they cast off everything that could potentially weigh them down. In the marathon of life, we must do the same by giving up the baggage of bitterness that would hold us back from reaching God's full potential for our lives.

3. We forgive because it helps the forgiven become a better person.

Think about what forgiveness has meant to you. When you have been forgiven, you've felt like a new person with a fresh beginning, right? Now think about the effect forgiveness can have in your marriage. When you choose to let go of bitterness or resentment toward your husband—even if you think you have a right to feel that way—your spouse gets a fresh beginning. He is free to make new choices, better ones.

The risk you take is that he may choose to continue in the fault or sin. But the fact is, unforgiveness always stifles and stagnates. Forgiveness, while risky, carries with it an enormous potential for healing and growth.

When we became Christians, our sins were forgiven through Christ, and we started a new life. Paul put it this way: "If anyone is in Christ, he is a new creation; the old has gone, the new has come! All this is from God, who reconciled us to himself through Christ and gave us the ministry of reconciliation" (2 Corinthians 5:17–18). As forgiven creatures, we have experienced the refreshment, joy, and newness that reconciliation brings. Let's extend that same opportunity to our husbands.

But How Do I Forgive?

No one said forgiveness would be easy. In fact, it is quite possibly one of the most difficult roads you and I will ever travel. It may require continued perseverance, a daily overcoming of great pain, and a constant effort to keep moving forward away from bitterness. More often

There's no point in burying a hatchet if you're going to put up a marker on the site. —Sydney Harris

than not, it will require a strength beyond our own—God's strength. Our human tendency is to want a step-by-step formula to easy forgiveness. But formulas won't work because each opportunity to forgive involves different circumstances and different people. Instead of a formula, I want to present some general principles of forgiveness that can be applied to most situations.

Recognize. Sometimes we don't even notice that the dirty demon of anger and bitterness has crept in the back door of our hearts. The attitude of unforgiveness can be quite insidious. That's why it's important for us to take inventory periodically to identify any grudges we are holding against our husbands or anyone else.

Often we get so busy with our daily routines that we don't take the time for that kind of reflection. I've personally found the Sabbath day to be a good time to reflect on my relationships and do a "forgiveness check." God's intention in setting aside one day each week as holy was to give us time for spiritual, physical, and emotional renewal. Few things bring a greater sense of renewal than the act of releasing our hurts and extending forgiveness.

Let me encourage you to set aside time on a regular basis to do a forgiveness check. Ask God to reveal any unforgiveness between you and your husband that needs to be healed and made right.

Realize. In order to forgive our husbands, we must realize three things. First, because of what Jesus did for us on the cross, we have no right to hold a grudge over the head of another person. Through the power of the blood of Christ, we have been forgiven much. Our grateful response is to forgive others as we have been forgiven.

Second, everyone falls. We may not fall in the same place or the same way or even as frequently as our husbands do, but we do fall. Just as we need the warm hand of forgiveness extended to us, so we are to extend grace and mercy to our spouses and others.

Third, we must realize that we are dependent on God's power to forgive. We are human; when we've been hurt or wronged, we struggle with strong feelings of anger and bitterness and the desire for revenge. In our own strength, we will always have trouble with forgiving. We need God's strength.

How do you receive God's power and strength to forgive? By asking for it. Consider praying a prayer similar to this one. Insert your husband's name in the blanks:

Dear Lord, I know that I need to forgive _____, but what he has done doesn't deserve forgiveness. Then again, none of us deserve forgiveness. Thank you for your grace. Thank you for your forgiveness through Christ's blood. Help me through the power of your Holy Spirit to forgive _____. Give me the strength to make a conscious decision to forgive him and move on. I am weak, but you are strong. Pour out your forgiving love through me. Work in _____'s life to help him become a new person and use my forgiveness as a step in the process. In Jesus' name, amen.

Release. Picture a heavy bucket filled with all the disappointments, wrongs, and mistakes you hold against your spouse: being late for dinner one too many times, throwing dirty socks on the floor, buying a cheap present on your anniversary, making a poor investment and losing money in the stock market, forgetting to take out the trash or walk the dog, failing to go to church; the list could go on and on. Imagine yourself holding this bucket over your husband's head. Now mentally take that bucket and walk over to the guardrail of an imaginary ship far out on the ocean. Hold the bucket out over the water and let it drop. Let it go! Free yourself from the weight of those sources of anger and frustration.

The truth is, the bucket was never your responsibility to hold in the first place. Psalm 103:12 says, "As far as the east is from the west, so far has [God] removed our transgressions from us." You and I must do the same for our spouses.

Resume. I think it's safe to assume that most of us weren't holding a huge bucket of anger and resentment over our husbands' heads when we first got married. I'm guessing that you, like me, had overlooked your husband's faults and weaknesses and saw only a glowing groom on your wedding day. We all started marriage with an empty bucket. But things changed, and over time that bucket began to fill up.

As we release our heavy buckets into the deep blue sea of forgiveness, we must resume our marriage relationships from the position of a clean slate. This can be hard to do in our own strength. But our very weakness gives us the opportunity to allow God's power to work through us.

Forgiveness must be reflected in our actions. Remember our study of Romans 12 in chapter 1? In verses 17 and 18 we read, "Never pay back evil for evil to anyone. Do things in such a way that everyone can see you are honorable. Do your part to live in peace with everyone, as much as possible." Then in verse 21: "Don't let evil get the best of you, but conquer evil by doing good" (NLT).

Start right now to do the actions it takes to resume your relationship with your husband. Speak kindly to him. Come alongside him as his complement and build him up. Help him to be the person God created him to be. Bless him, don't curse him.

After all, what good is it to say with our mouths that we forgive our spouses if we show no evidence of it in our actions? I think of a woman I know—let's call her Sandy—who says she forgives her husband and even quotes Bible verses about forgiveness. But she also says awful things about him behind his back, and she is rude and angry to his face. It's obvious to everyone around her that she has never really emptied her bucket. Actions always speak volumes when it comes to love and forgiveness. We must heed the words in 1 John 3:18: "Dear children, let us not love with words or tongue but with actions and in truth."

Take responsibility. Forgiveness doesn't take away consequences or negate responsibility. In loving and forgiving, we must also help the one we've forgiven to be a better person. If a husband is continually unfaithful or constantly running the family into debt or caught in the trap of substance abuse, he can be forgiven; but he must also learn to live responsibly. Continual sin indicates the need for help, and our forgiveness should not be an enabler to further sin. Responsibility is demanded on the part of both the forgiver and the forgiven. Yes, we must forgive our husbands completely in our hearts and minds. But then, if we see them mired in habitual or continual sin, we must love them enough to help them get out of it.

Although ultimate restoration is in God's hands, we have certain responsibilities. (Of course, if abuse is involved, our responsibility is to remove ourselves—and our children—from the situation.) Paul wrote to the Galatians, "Brothers, if someone is caught in a sin, you who are spiritual should restore him gently. But watch yourself, or you also may be tempted. Carry each other's burdens, and in this way you will fulfill the law of Christ" (Galatians 6:1–2). Jesus addressed the same issue in Matthew 18:15–17:

> If your brother sins against you, go and show him his fault, just between the two of you. If he listens to you, you have won your brother over. But if he will not listen, take one or two others along, so that "every matter may be established by the testimony of two or three witnesses." If he refuses to listen to them, tell it to the church;

and if he refuses to listen even to the church, treat him as you would a pagan or a tax collector.

The challenge for many of us wives is to remember that we are not our husband's Holy Spirit. It is not our calling to be Holy Nags! But if your husband is caught in a habitual sin, help him. Direct your love and forgiveness toward his restoration. Walk the road to recovery with him hand in hand. Of course, each marriage has its own unique set of circumstances. I cannot and should not tell you what to do in every situation involving a spouse's destructive behavior or continual sin. But in most cases, these four resources can be helpful:

1. *A godly Christian counselor* who uses the Bible as his or her primary resource. If your husband won't go with you, visit the counselor on your own to learn how best to respond to your spouse and help him achieve victory. A counselor can also help you decide if intervention is necessary.

2. *Strong and responsible Christian friends* who are willing to meet regularly with your husband, ask the tough questions, and hold him accountable. (Of course, your spouse must be willing to submit to that accountability.)

3. *Good reading material.* For both wisdom and encouragement, I strongly recommend the following books: *How to Act Right When Your Spouse Acts Wrong* by Leslie Vernick (WaterBrook Press, 2001); *Love Must Be Tough* by Dr. James Dobson (Word Publishing Group, 1996); and *The Art of Forgiving* by Lewis B. Smedes (Ballantine Books, 1996).

4. *Prayer.* Praying for your husband is your highest calling and most important responsibility as his wife. Habitual sin represents

a spiritual battle. You can faithfully fight that battle using the spiritual weapon of prayer.

Before we move on, allow me to gently ask two questions. First, could it be that *you* are the one who is caught in habitual sin, and your husband is the one sitting in the seat of forgiveness? If so, please talk to your spouse, consider the four resources we've mentioned, and take action to get help together. The journey to recovery is not an easy road, but I guarantee it will be a healing road for both you and your husband.

Second, are you holding on to bitterness toward people from your childhood or some other time in your past? A marriage suffers not only when the spouses harbor unforgiveness toward one another; it also suffers when one or both partners hold unforgiveness in their hearts toward people who were in their lives before their wedding day.

For example, many of us find it easy to blame our parents for our shortcomings. We coddle anger and resentment toward them well into adulthood, using their sins or weaknesses as an excuse to live our own defeated lives. We need to let go of the anger and the excuses—along with any right we think we have to hold our parents' faults over their heads. They are sinful people in need of forgiveness just like the rest of us. If you are maintaining an unforgiving heart toward your parents or anyone else from your past, the person you're hurting the most is you. You're also hurting your spouse, who must deal with the effects of your attitude of unforgiveness. Why not experience the joy and peace that forgiveness brings? Begin the healing process today!

Queens of Forgiveness

History tells us that King Louis XII of France had many enemies before ascending to the throne. When he became king, those who had opposed him were filled with fear. You see, Louis had composed a list of his enemies and had placed a black cross next to each name. The men on the list didn't know what the black cross meant; but assuming the worst, they lost no time getting as far away from Paris as possible.

Imagine their astonishment when each man was recalled from his retreat and assured that he had been pardoned by the king! The black cross placed by the side of each man's name, it turned out, was not the mark of punishment or death as they had supposed; rather, it was a symbol of forgiveness. The black cross reminded the king that, just as he had received forgiveness from God through the shed blood of Jesus on the cross, so he must forgive others. His example was Christ, who could have summoned a legion of angels to assist and avenge him but chose instead to pray for his murderers, saying, "Father, forgive them; for they know not what they do."[4]

As positive wives and queens in our homes, we can have the same royal attitude. We have been forgiven by Christ. Now let's follow his example and forgive all those around us—especially our husbands.

POWER POINT

⚙ **Read:** Matthew 26:31–35, 69–75; John 21:1–17. How do you think Peter felt about his actions on the night Jesus was betrayed? Why do you think Jesus questioned Peter three times in the passage in John? What indication do you have that Jesus truly forgave Peter?

♡ **Pray:** Glorious Lord and forgiving Father, how wonderful is your love toward me! I cannot begin to know its height or depth, but I do know that nothing can separate me from that love. Thank you for your love and for the forgiveness you have provided through the death of your Son, Jesus, on the cross. Thank you that he died and rose again, giving me the promise of forgiveness and eternal life. Help me now to pour this forgiveness out to everyone around me, and especially to my husband. Give me the strength and the ability to forgive. Help me to move on and not hold grudges. Allow me to release any resentment I have toward my spouse, and help me to love him by forgiving him as I have been forgiven. In Jesus' name, amen.

💡 **Remember:** "Be kind and compassionate to one another, forgiving each other, just as in Christ God forgave you" (Ephesians 4:32).

☺ **Do:** Set aside a time this coming weekend to rest and reflect, and pray for God to reveal any areas of unforgiveness in your heart. Then walk through the process we discussed in this chapter: *recognize* the unforgiveness, *realize* you have no right to hold on to it, *release* bitterness and anger, *resume* your relationship with a clean slate, and help *restore* your spouse if he is caught in destructive behavior patterns or habitual sin.

Power Principle #2

THe Power OF Commitment

Marriage is a promise that is shared by only two—
a vow to love and dream and plan together all life through.

—Louis Fromm

*May the Lord direct your hearts into God's love
and Christ's perseverance.*

—2 Thessalonians 3:5

A Rare Commodity
Lasting Loyalty in a "Greener Grass" Society

*You have to walk carefully in the beginning of love; the running
across fields into your lover's arms can only come later
when you're sure they won't laugh if you trip.*

—Jonathan Carroll

A precious family of doves makes its home each year on the top of a pillar on our back porch. It is our pleasure to watch them from our breakfast-room window as they fly back and forth, preparing the nest. Within a couple of weeks, we begin to hear the sweet chirping of tiny, fledgling doves emerging from the safety of their little shells. Now and then we catch a glimpse of their squawking mouths begging for food. And then of course comes the thrill of seeing these young ones take flight. We feel almost as though these are our own little babies leaving to find a new home.

Perhaps we love watching these doves so much because many years ago, Curt and I raised a pair of beautiful, white pet doves. We enjoyed watching our birds grow, mature, nest, and even have a little baby dove of their own. It was a sad day in the Ladd household when the male dove met an untimely death from a predator. But it was even sadder for the dove left behind.

The female soon began to act sickly, and I couldn't seem to get her to eat anything. Within days she passed away too. I was shocked and saddened and wanted to understand what had happened to her. In my research I quickly discovered that our precious pets were, in fact, "mourning doves." I had thought the title was *morning*, as in the early hours of the day when they awakened us with their cooing. But no, *mourning* is the correct spelling. Mourning doves mate for life, and when one dies, the spouse is always quick to follow. My female dove died of a broken heart.

What an incredible picture of commitment! If only we saw this same quality in human beings (not the mourn-yourself-to-death part; the mate-for-life part). In our culture, sad to say, our commitment level has diminished to the point that most of us commit only to what's convenient. Statistics tell us, for example, that the divorce rate for all married couples in America currently stands at 54 percent; and according to one study, 70 percent of those divorces were probably "needless." In other words, these couples didn't divorce because of physical abuse, substance abuse, or infidelity, but rather because of issues such as immaturity, changes in lifestyle, or incompatibility.[1] Their commitment to their marriages vanished when it became inconvenient.

Essentials

Commitment is a form of glue that holds a marriage together. Often we say that love is the glue; but it's our commitment to one another and our dedication to our marriage vows that actually seal the covenant. Love and commitment are similar in some ways, but they are not the same. When we say we love someone, there is an assumption of commitment; but when we say we are committed to someone, love may or may not be present. You *can* have commitment without love. Most of the time, however, the two go hand in hand.

Perhaps the biggest difference between love and commitment is that love is an attitude of the heart and a decision of the will; commitment is an issue of character. When I say I will meet someone at a certain place on a particular day, it is a matter of character that I hold to my word. The same is true when I say I will serve on a committee at my children's school or carry out an obligation at work. When I say I will do something, I should do it. That's commitment based on the integrity of my word.

A Vow Is a Vow

When we make a vow or take an oath, we commit ourselves; we give our word that we will do what we say we will do. In most marriage vows, for example, we pledge to love, honor, and cherish each other "until death do us part." But statistics show that many of us don't follow through. These days people stay in marriage until "my needs aren't being met" or "we just don't get along."

Claiming "irreconcilable differences" is the easy way out. Every couple has differences! What people ought to say is, "We can't seem to overlook our differences anymore, so we give up." If we were honest, the courts would have a stamp to place on divorce judgments that says, "Lack of Commitment." Of course, "Irreconcilable Differences" seems much more pleasant, because it doesn't call anyone's character into question. "Lack of Commitment" implies that we don't keep our word, and that's not a pretty picture.

What are the reasons for the lack of commitment in marriage today? Certainly one factor is the increase in dishonesty and general devaluing of integrity that has taken place in modern society. Our culture has moved far from honoring truth. There was a day when it was noble to keep your word; nowadays, we're not the least bit surprised when someone doesn't. In 1844 Ralph Waldo Emerson wrote, "Truth is the summit of being."[2] Yet by 1922 Christopher Morley could aptly say, "Truth is not a diet but a condiment."[3] Isn't it sad to think how quickly we moved from valuing truth as an essential character trait to considering it an "extra"? Think how much further that value has fallen since 1922!

Jesus was well aware of the condition of the human heart and the challenges we face when it comes to keeping our commitments. In the Sermon on the Mount, he charged:

> It has been said, "Anyone who divorces his wife must give her a certificate of divorce." But I tell you that anyone who divorces his wife, except for marital unfaithfulness, causes her to become an adulteress, and anyone who marries the divorced woman commits adultery. Again, you have heard that it was said to the people long ago, "Do not break your oath, but keep the oaths you have made to the Lord." But I tell you, Do not swear at all: either by heaven, for it is God's throne; or by the earth, for it is his footstool; or by Jerusalem, for it is the city of the Great King. And do not swear by your head, for you cannot make even one hair white or black. Simply let your "Yes" be "Yes," and your "No," "No"; anything beyond this comes from the evil one. (Matthew 5:31–37)

Would you say that Jesus had some strong ideas about the power of a vow? Clearly, rescinding a vow is no light matter—especially a vow of marriage. Going back on our marriage vows is a breaking of our word in the grandest sense. We didn't just speak our vows to our husbands; we stood before both God and men and made a public commitment.

Unfortunately, while God expects us to keep our vows, people generally don't. You've probably heard the joke that says the amount of money spent on a wedding is in inverse proportion to how long the marriage will actually last. Recently I heard someone say that 60 percent of all guests who come to a wedding to witness a couple's vows secretly believe the marriage is doomed to failure. I'm not so sure how anyone could come up with that statistic, short of a wedding exit poll.

But the bold implication is that we have lost confidence in the ability of our fellow humans to keep a marriage vow. We need look no further than Hollywood—where the most common question is, "Is this her fourth or fifth marriage?"—to see that this is true.

Happy or Holy?

The devaluing of our word has definitely been a destructive factor in marriage, but it probably accounts for only a fraction of the true reason so many marriages today end in "needless" divorce. A more dominant reason, I'm convinced, is the mistaken belief that says, "Marriage is supposed to make me happy, and if I'm not happy, then I must get out." Think back to your own courtship and early marriage. Didn't you think that your spouse was there to love you and cherish you and make you happy? (I did!) That blissful thought permeates our culture.

But the truth is, it's a mumpsimus. I call it the marriage mumpsimus —probably the biggest and most widespread mistaken belief in the world today. In his book *Sacred Marriage*, Gary Thomas challenges the marriage mumpsimus with this question: "What if God designed marriage to make us holy more than to make us happy?"[4] What a novel idea in today's world!

The reality is, people aren't easy to live with. As Christians, we're called to recognize that fact and then persevere through the tough times, whether we feel "happy" or not. We were never promised "easy" in life. Quite the contrary; we are warned in Scripture that life is not going to be so great all the time.

The early Christians knew what perseverance was all about. Paul wrote to Timothy in 2 Timothy 2:3, "Endure hardship with us like a good soldier of Christ Jesus." The first-century Christians understood the cost of commitment. Many gave their very lives for the cause of Christ. And here *we* are, whining, "But he's so insensitive" or "He just

We can do whatever we wish to do provided our wish is strong enough. —Katherine Mansfield ☺

doesn't understand me" or "He spends too much money"! Our Christian forefathers and mothers must be disgusted to see our wimpy commitment level.

Please don't misunderstand me. If a wife is in a physically abusive relationship, she should definitely remove herself from the situation and get help. But at the very least, a marriage commitment *should* give us the motivation to endure those little idiosyncrasies or traits we don't particularly like or enjoy about our husbands. It *should* give us the perseverance to hang in there through the tough times that are inevitable in every marriage.

As Gary Thomas suggested, maybe God's primary goal for us is not happiness, but making us more like Jesus. And maybe perseverance in marriage is one of the tools God wants to use to conform us to his image. And maybe true happiness and joy come not from pursuing our own pleasure or good but from obeying God and seeking first his kingdom.

What would happen if we looked at our spouses' differences and our marital difficulties and asked ourselves, "What does God want me to learn from this relationship? How does he want me to grow in this situation in order to make me more like Christ?" What if we went on to inquire, "How can I be a complement to my husband in his weakness? How can I be a blessing to him in this circumstance?" Wouldn't it be wonderful to begin to look at our husbands with compassion and encouragement instead of disgust and frustration? Wouldn't we all be a lot happier?

We Are Not Alone

Most of us take comfort from knowing we're not the only ones going through a particular difficulty. I remember when, as a young mother, I found out that other young mothers struggled with discipline problems and temper tantrums. That "Oh, you do too?" moment was so consoling! Unfortunately, so many of us show up at church on Sunday mornings with plastic smiles and standard responses—"Just fine, how are you?"—that we often think we're the only ones struggling with marriage issues. Cheer up, sister! The fact of the matter is, whenever two sinful people join together as one flesh, there are going to be problems—some more pronounced than others, to be sure; but we all have them. If any wife says her marriage is problem free, she's either lying or she has been married only two days.

Our challenges as wives come in all shapes and sizes. For some marriages the big issue is money; others struggle with trust or sex or communication. Typically, a wife feels misunderstood; that just goes with the territory. Why? Because God created men and women differently, and generally speaking, we don't think alike. Do you think your husband is insensitive? Join the club! With a few exceptions, most men are not wired to be particularly sensitive to a woman's feelings. Sorry to tell you this, but—to put it bluntly—you're going to have to adjust. Just as much as you want to be understood, your husband wants you to understand that he can't understand you. Did you follow that?

We shouldn't be surprised when challenges come our way. They are normal, and many are common to most marriages. Instead, as positive wives we must choose to love *through* the difficulties and *past* the differences. We must make a conscious choice to overlook our husbands' faults and focus on their potential. (We'll talk more about how to do this in chapter 8.) Marriage is a lifetime commitment. We can't give up just because challenges exist!

Psychologist John Gottman claims that he can predict whether a couple will "stay happily together or lose their way." From his research he concludes, "Happily married couples aren't smarter, richer, or more psychologically astute than others. But in their day-to-day lives, they have hit upon a dynamic that keeps their negative thoughts and feelings about each other (which all couples have) from overwhelming their positive ones."[5] In other words, they choose to see more of the good in one another and less of the bad. Why do some couples do this so well, while others struggle? I'm sure it's because they have anchored themselves in the foundational belief that marriage is for life, and they know they must make the best of it.

I began this section with the heading "We Are Not Alone." That phrase has two meanings. First, we are not alone because *every* marriage experiences some degree of struggle. There are other women who are going through struggles similar to those we're going through. And second, we are not alone because we have a wonderful, loving God. His love toward us endures, giving us the motivation and the impetus to pour out that same enduring love to our husbands.

Do you feel that you just can't overlook your husband's glaring faults? Take those faults before the Father. Ask God to help you see past them and grow through them. Ask him to show you gentle—not nagging—ways to be a complement and a help to your spouse. By all means, pray for your husband's flaws to diminish, but be sure to include a prayer for your own flaws as well.

No Backdoor Policy

Do you remember the day you first discovered a naughty word— you know, a "cussword"? I'll never forget the day my sister, Karen, and I were sitting in the backseat of the car as our mother was pulling out of the driveway. Our windows were rolled down, and a neighbor boy artfully threw (perhaps I should say gracefully chucked) a crumpled-up piece of paper through the open window into my sister's lap.

Karen, who was just barely reading age, proceeded to uncrumple the paper and read out loud the one word that was printed on it. I won't tell you what the word was. Suffice it to say, when it passed over my sister's lips, my mother was horrified! At first she was angry with Karen. But when she figured out what had happened, she became positively enraged at the neighbor boy who'd had the gall to throw the paper—and that word—into our car. Fortunately for him, he was long gone by the time my mother understood the whole story.

But wait, it gets worse. In fact, the incident I'm about to describe has been entered into my mother's list of most embarrassing moments. You see, we were in the car in the first place because we were headed to the grocery store. (Are you getting nervous?) As we went down the crowded aisles of the grocery store, one of us (Karen and I still debate over which one) asked in an unrestrained tone, "Mom, what does _____ mean?"

You can imagine the reaction of my sweet, mild-mannered mother at this point. How do you explain to a crowd of people stopped in their tracks and staring at you in the grocery store, "A neighbor boy threw a piece of paper with that word on it through our car window and she just learned the word and she doesn't know what it means and we never use that word in our home and she will never use it again and I'm so sorry she said it just now." Of course, our curiosity about the word increased in direct proportion to the intensity of my mother's attempts to squelch our interest. Needless to say, we left the store without completing our grocery list.

Certain words should never be added to our verbal vocabularies. Thanks to a troublemaking neighbor, Karen and I discovered one of them at an early age. When I was engaged to Curt, a very wise and wonderful woman taught me another one. The one word that should never be uttered in a marriage relationship, she said, is the D word: *divorce*. We must never let it roll off our tongues.

Why? Because speaking the word *divorce* is the key that unlocks the back door of our marriages. In the heat of the moment, during a fiery argument, it is a temptation to say the word. Don't do it! Words are a powerful force, and when you speak the D word, you throw a new concept into the window of your marriage. You imply that there is a way out—and you begin to think you can inch your way toward it. Except in cases of infidelity or abuse, the marriage vow is to be honored.

Keep this picture prominently in your mind's eye: There is no back door! Your marriage commitment is a vow to stay with your husband through thick and thin. You entered into a covenant, and you need to stick with it even when the road gets bumpy. If you have already allowed the D word into your home, let me encourage you: Get rid of it today! Just as a mother washes her child's mouth out with soap for saying something naughty, cleanse your relationship and purge it of that word. Agree with your spouse that the D word will never be uttered again.

Never Give Up

I'm a big Winston Churchill fan. He was an incredible leader and an inspiring statesman who strengthened and encouraged the English people during some of their most challenging years. Also a profound orator, Churchill is known for one of his greatest speeches that was a short one, but it packed a powerful punch. Here's what he said: "Never give in, never give in, never, never, never, never—in nothing, great or small, large or petty—never give in except to convictions of honor and good sense."[6]

Sometimes it's not the length of the message that counts, but the content. To his audience, Churchill's brief address was life giving and invaluable, and it still resonates with us today. Are you willing to heed its call? Through your husband's weaknesses, through his shortcomings, through his problems and yours, are you willing to never give up? Are you willing to live for eternity and not for the moment?

In 1 Corinthians 13:8 Paul proclaims, "Love never fails." He goes on to list things that will pass away—prophecies, tongues, knowledge. But faith, hope, and love, he says, will endure; and "the greatest of these is love" (1 Corinthians 13:13). Do you feel like giving up on your marriage? Don't! Have faith that God can help you through your current struggle. Hold on to the hope that God can resurrect even the deadest of marriages. Most of all, allow God's redeeming love to pour into you and fill the emptiness in your heart. You *can* choose to never, never, never give in. God's love, poured into you and then through you, never fails.

POWER POINT

⚙ **Read:** Highlights from Abraham and Sarah's marriage in Genesis 12:1–6, 10–20; 20:1–17; 21:1–5. Name some of the challenges Abraham and Sarah had in their marriage. What mistakes did Abraham make? What evidence do we see that Sarah endured hardship?

🕊 **Pray:** Eternal heavenly Father, thank you for never giving up on me. Your love is relentless and enduring! Thank you for loving me through all my faults and failures. May my love for my husband persevere too. Renew our marriage, and help us to recommit ourselves to one another for a lifetime. Keep us faithful to our marriage vows until death do us part. Seal our marriage with your undying love, forgiveness, hope, and perseverance. In Jesus' name I pray, amen.

💡 **Remember:** "Let us not become weary in doing good, for at the proper time we will reap a harvest if we do not give up" (Galatians 6:9).

☺ **Do:** Write a love note to your husband. Tell him how glad you are to be married to him and list some of the qualities he possesses that make you thankful. Close the note by telling him you are committed to him for the rest of your life. Give him the note when he comes home from work, or send it to him at his workplace. (Be sure to mark it "confidential"!)

6

The Art of Arguing
Techniques and Tips for Positive Disagreement

Conflict is inevitable.
What matters is how it is handled.

—Michael J. McManus

Le Anne was in a hurry to finish icing the beautiful German chocolate cake she had baked for her mother-in-law's birthday. She felt a little under pressure, knowing that she had a load of laundry to finish, packages to wrap, and e-mail to check before loading the family into the car for the hour-long drive to the birthday celebration.

As she put the final touches on the frosting, her husband, Paul, walked in from his usual Saturday golf game with the guys. Taking one look at the cake, he declared, "That will never work."

"What?" Le Anne said in a not-so-friendly tone.

"My mother is allergic to pecans. She will puff up like a balloon if she eats the icing on that cake."

"Well, she can just eat around the icing," Le Anne snapped, "because I'm not making another cake!"

"You can't give her a birthday cake that she can't eat."

Le Anne turned and glared at her husband. "If you hadn't been out playing golf all day," she retorted, "you would have been here to tell me what kind of cake she *can* eat!"

Before long the issue was no longer pecans in the icing. It progressed quickly to Paul's regular weekend absences, his "obsession" with golf, and his inability to understand the strain and pressure of his wife's busy life. It finally ended with Le Anne's buying a cake at the local grocery store and not speaking one word to Paul all the way to his mother's house. I suppose he's lucky that she even went!

Sound semifamiliar? Change the names and a few details, and that scene is one that has played out in all of our lives. Oh, the petty things that lead to major blowouts in a marriage!

There is no denying the fact that all couples disagree from time to time. Conflicts flare up in every marriage for any number of reasons, great or small. And while we might assume that husbands and wives who argue a lot are more likely to head to divorce court than couples who argue less frequently, research published by The Christophers, a nonprofit organization based in New York City, notes that divorcing couples typically don't argue any more than successful couples do. From the data, The Christophers conclude that the key to success or failure in marriage is not *how many* disagreements a couple has, but rather *how* they disagree.[1]

Marital conflict may be natural, but it doesn't have to be messy. There is an art to successful arguing. As positive wives, we need to learn the proper techniques so that our inevitable disagreements with our husbands lead to understanding rather than division. We need to learn how to fight fair. That's what this chapter is all about.

Is It Worth the Fight?

Before we get into the specific dos and don'ts of arguing, let's agree on one point: Not every argument is worth the fight. Now, I'm not suggesting we set a limit on the number of arguments we can have. ("Oops, that's the third argument this week. We've reached our quota. Any new disagreements will have to be taken up on Monday.") But there *is* wisdom in choosing not to take every issue to battle. Some things are worth fighting for; some things are not.

Marriage, like all relationships, involves give and take. It's not all about what *we* like, what *we* want, what *we* need. Sometimes the best thing to do in a situation is to overlook our hurt, swallow our pride, and set aside our own needs and desires. As Ellen Fein and Sherrie Schneider write in their book *The Rules for Marriage,* there are certain things that we ought to simply let go. "Life is not fair. Don't be a bean-counter, keeping score of everything you do versus what he does," they advise.[2] Sometimes we must give up our "rights" for what *is* right.

Our guidebook for life, the Bible, says a lot about our rights when it comes to handling conflict. For example, Jesus tells us to turn the other cheek when someone offends us (Matthew 5:39). He teaches that we are to be peacemakers (Matthew 5:9). He also says that if a brother sins against us, we should go to him, show him his fault, and try to resolve the issue (Matthew 18:15). The apostle Paul echoes this theme when he says that, as much as possible, we should live at peace with everyone (Romans 12:18). He addresses the issue of "rights" in many of his letters to the early church. Let's look at a couple of key verses.

> Do everything without complaining or arguing, so that you may become blameless and pure, children of God without fault in a crooked and depraved generation, in which you shine like stars in the universe as you hold out the word of life—in order that I may boast on the day of Christ that I did not run or labor for nothing. But even if I am being poured out like a drink offering on the sacrifice and service coming from your faith, I am glad and rejoice with all of you. So you too should be glad and rejoice with me. (Philippians 2:14–18)

> But whatever was to my profit I now consider loss for the sake of Christ. What is more, I consider everything a loss compared to the

surpassing greatness of knowing Christ Jesus my Lord, for whose sake I have lost all things. I consider them rubbish, that I may gain Christ and be found in him, not having a righteousness of my own that comes from the law, but that which is through faith in Christ—the righteousness that comes from God and is by faith. (Philippians 3:7–9)

These verses remind us to have an eternal perspective—to recognize that this life on earth is not the only kingdom for which we live. Things that seem like big issues to us are often of little consequence when we consider them in light of the big picture. Winning an argument and getting what we want may feel good in the short term, but we gain more in the long run if we follow the examples of Jesus and Paul and lay down our lives—and our rights—for others.

That's not to say we should never argue with our spouses. There *are* times to stand up for what we want or need. There are times to bring up a hurt or frustration and discuss it. If a particular issue is going to continue to bother us, we shouldn't overlook it. It is better to discuss a matter than to allow it to fester and grow into a bigger problem. Making our husbands aware of our interests, needs, and desires is healthy. But creating a war over those interests, needs, and desires is, more often than not, both unhealthy and unnecessary.

Let's say that Amy wants to redecorate the living room, but Steve feels the room is fine the way it is and doesn't see any need for drastic change. Amy could dig in her heels, whine, complain, nag, and argue until she gets her way. But is it really worth the war? A better approach might be to consider her husband's position and ask herself some questions. For example: What are Steve's main objections? Can we afford to redecorate right now? What are the benefits of redecorating, and what actually needs to be done? Are my motives pure, or am I simply trying to keep up with the Joneses? Could I wait a while? Are there some simple changes that both Steve and I can agree to? After Amy takes the time to pray and carefully evaluate the situation, she will be in a much better position to discuss her hopes and desires with Steve in a positive way.

We must remember that every dream is not meant to become a reality in this life. Most of us have said at one time or another, "I have always wanted _____." (You fill in the blank.) But just because we have "always wanted" something doesn't mean we were meant to have it or need to demand it. God has created us in such a way that our greatest dreams and desires can only be fulfilled in our heavenly home. I'm not saying we must give up all our earthly interests and desires; I'm saying we must be willing at times to die to our own self-interest and live for our future home, not this current one.

James gives us good advice: "My dear brothers, take note of this: Everyone should be quick to listen, slow to speak and slow to become angry, for man's anger does not bring about the righteous life that God desires. Therefore, get rid of all moral filth and the evil that is so prevalent and humbly accept the word planted in you, which can save you" (James 1:19–21). When it comes down to it, very few issues demand disagreement. Here is a short list to consider:

- Disobedience to God (for example, adultery, uncontrolled anger, lying)

- Disobedience to the law (cheating on taxes, continually overspending or going into debt, driving while intoxicated, using illegal drugs, and so on)

- Harm to yourself or others (physical or verbal abuse aimed at you, your children, or other family members)

Although we may have the right—and even the obligation—to disagree in such situations, we must still do so in a respectful and positive way. But let's be honest. Most of the arguments we have with our

Let us therefore make every effort to do what leads to peace and to mutual edification. —Romans 14:19

husbands don't involve the issues we've just named, do they? Rather, they erupt in the heat of the moment over smaller, often petty issues that have been stoked into flame by a myriad of back issues we've allowed to smolder over time.

Rules of Engagement

Most of the time an argument just "happens." We're not expecting it, we don't necessarily want it, and we don't have the opportunity to plan it out in advance. Often it becomes quite emotional, and we end up doing or saying things we later regret. That's why, if we're going to be positive wives, we need to have some predetermined rules of engagement. Here is "The Positive Wife's List of Conflict Dos and Don'ts":

Do

- Listen more than you talk. (James 1:19)
- Remain calm; keep your voice down. (Proverbs 15:1)
- Keep current; leave old issues behind. (Philippians 3:13)
- Avoid condescending phrases or character attacks. (Ephesians 4:29–32)
- Stick with facts, not speculations. (2 Corinthians 10:5)
- Be ready and willing to ask for forgiveness or offer it. (Colossians 3:13)
- Speak clearly, thoughtfully, and respectfully. (Colossians 4:6)
- Guard your tongue from saying something you will regret later. (James 3:9–10)
- Pray together. (1 Thessalonians 5:17)
- Get to the point. (1 Timothy 6:20)

Don't

- Don't ever use the D word (divorce).

- Don't use phrases such as "you always" or "you never."

- Don't shout or scream.

- Don't give the silent treatment.

- Don't lie or manipulate.

- Don't beg or cry.

- Don't push his hot buttons.

- Don't bring up past sins or hurts.

Following these rules will help to ensure a fair fight and give us the best chance for achieving a positive resolution to our conflict. That resolution, however, does not have to come in the form of one winner and one loser. Actually, the best arguments have two results: a diminishing of the initial conflict and an understanding of one another's perspective. That's not win-lose; that's win-win.

Recently I was reading a list of one-liners sent to me over the Internet. One of them went like this: "If you do not understand someone, walk a mile in his shoes. Then you will have his shoes, and you will be a mile away from him." That's not the kind of resolution we want as positive wives! But I do think we need to put ourselves in our husbands' shoes more often and try to see things through their eyes. In a conflict we should seek not so much to win as to ensure that we and our husbands come to a better understanding of each other's point of view.

Sometimes we want to win so much that we won't let an issue go. I admit—and Curt can confirm—that I am an expert at beating a topic to a slow, cruel, and emotional death (although I am getting better at letting go). I've learned from experience that going over and over the same topic until you hack it to death is no way to argue. It's much better to set a mental time limit on a disagreement. That way, you're more likely to get right to the point and refrain from chasing rabbit trails of unrelated frustration or past pain. And just knowing that an argument *will* come to an end is a great comfort when you're in the middle of it.

Granted, most arguments erupt without any pre-planning, so you may have to set your time limit on the fly. Give a quick glance to your watch and make a mental decision to rest your case in, say, ten minutes—even if you haven't won. Keep in mind that the best way to end the argument may be to "agree to disagree." That's a perfectly valid resolution! Let me say it again: It's okay to resolve a dispute by agreeing to disagree with one another. If the issue warrants, you can agree to disagree for a set period of time and then schedule a time to revisit it. You might be amazed at how much your heart, mind, and desires can change when you've had an extended period to think and pray.

Timing Is Everything

Comedian Dave Barry gives this interesting description of time: "Aside from Velcro, time is the most mysterious substance in the universe. You can't see it or touch it, yet a plumber can charge you upwards of seventy-five dollars per hour for it, without necessarily fixing anything."[3] We may not be able to understand time or hold it in our hands; but as positive wives, we need to know enough about time to make wise use of it in our marriages.

When is the worst time to discuss a touchy issue or have a disagreement with your spouse? My husband can tell you, because I used to pick it much too often: bedtime. It's never wise to bring up an issue or pour out your hurts right before you go to bed. Ephesians 4:26 tells us not to let the sun go down on our anger. We should handle issues and problems during the day, not after the sun goes down and everyone is tired and irritable. If you think your husband is insensitive to your feelings, watch that insensitivity escalate as bedtime approaches. Why? Because all he wants to do is go to sleep. The last thing he wants to do when his head hits the pillow is discuss a difficult issue, especially if emotions are going to be in the mix.

When you need to approach your husband about a matter that may prompt disagreement, choose your timing wisely. If necessary, set an appointment. Say, "Honey, I know that bedtime is not the best time to start a discussion, and I really need to talk with you. Can we agree to talk tomorrow at 6:45, right after dinner?"

Always go to bed in peace, even if that means setting aside your anger and frustration for the night. You may find that your emotions are not as charged and the issue doesn't seem as big after a good night's rest. I know that whenever I take my anxious or angry thoughts to the Lord and allow them to wait overnight, they seem less intense the next day.

Time of day is not the only variable to consider in timing a discussion with your spouse; time of month is important too. Have you noticed there are certain times during a typical month when your husband can leave his dirty socks on the floor, complain about the spot in the carpet, forget to take out the trash, and show you less attention than he shows the remote control—and it's no big deal? Then there are other times during the month when he can make one slight implication about the quality of the evening meal, and you fall apart and give him a thirty-minute lecture about how to be kind and sensitive to a person's feelings—and it's *not* a pleasant lecture.

I know I've been there, and I have a feeling you've been there too. What is the underlying factor that prompts our reactions? Two words: fluctuating hormones. During the downside of our monthly cycles, hormonal changes can make us feel unloved and unsure of ourselves. In her book *Women and Stress,* Jean Lush lists a variety of symptoms that can surface during this time, including feelings of despair, negative attitudes toward ourselves and others, impulsiveness, fatigue, and a sense of loss.[4] The good news is, these symptoms usually subside after a few days.

But during those few particular days, we don't always handle things well. It's easy for us to blow matters out of proportion. Does that mean we can use hormones as an excuse to do damage to our marriage relationships? Absolutely not! Rather, we must recognize the part that hormones play in our lives and adjust to it.

For example, I have learned to get a little extra rest during my touchy time of the month. Lightening my schedule and taking time to do things that refresh me (such as reading a good book, taking a walk, or getting a neck massage) are often just what the doctor ordered to keep me from going over the top.

I have also found it helpful to warn Curt when I am struggling with my hormones. I put a sign in the bathroom that reads, "Hormone Alert—Proceed with Caution." This is my way of letting him know that he needs to be a little more gentle than usual with me and refrain from asking such questions as, "So what in the world did you do all day?" It's also my way of reminding him that if I get mad at something, he shouldn't be too quick to take it personally. My problem may not be him; it may be my hormones.

That doesn't mean I have a green light to go ballistic if Curt says something that angers me. It's not okay for me to scream, "Didn't you read the sign? Leave me alone. I'm hormonal!" Posting a sign doesn't give me permission to act like an ugly, green, husband-eating alien. But it does help to create more understanding between us.

As positive wives, we need to do whatever it takes to achieve harmony with our husbands and our hormones. If you struggle with intense PMS or have reached your menopausal years, you may want to consult a physician or look at alternative methods of hormone replace-ment. And if you become enraged with your husband over a simple issue or find yourself making a mountain out of a simple pile of dirt, take a deep breath—then go check the calendar. Maybe the problem is yours, not his.

Us against Them

One of my favorite movies of all time is *Iron Will.* It's based on the true story of a teenage boy named Will who took on the challenge of a North American transcontinental dogsled race. The audience follows Will through times of great danger. We see his emotional highs. We watch with anticipation as he battles blizzards, fatigue, and the devious actions of his enemy—a competitor who wants to win at any cost. But hurray for our hero! In one of those epic movie moments, the enemy's dogs fight amongst themselves and even turn on the villain. And as you can guess, Will flies off to victory.

Why did Will win the race? Because his dogs worked together to pull his sled over the long miles of rugged terrain. They worked as a team and moved in unison all the way to the finish line. Meanwhile, the dogs pulling the competitor's sled did not work together to the end. They turned on each other and made themselves, not the other racers, their own worst enemy.

As positive wives we must stay unified with our husbands to defeat the enemy. And who is our enemy? Peter tells us, "Be self-controlled and alert. Your enemy the devil prowls around like a roaring lion look-ing for someone to devour" (1 Peter 5:8). Satan would love to dissolve our marriages because they are a picture of Christ and the church. Marriage is God's design and institution, offering a spiritual and moral foundation for our culture. Yet the enemy often uses temptations from the current culture to attack and destroy our marriage bonds. Paul addresses this spiritual battle in Ephesians 6:10–12: "Finally, be strong in the Lord and in his mighty power. Put on the full armor of God so that you can take your stand against the devil's schemes. For our struggle is not against flesh and blood, but against the rulers, against the authorities, against the powers of this dark world and against the spiritual forces of evil in the heavenly realms."

When an issue comes between you and your husband, try to see the matter with spiritual eyes. Your husband is not the enemy; Satan is. Join with your husband and work together, in unison, to find a resolution to the challenge that is threatening you. I love what Benjamin Franklin said as our American forefathers pulled together against their common enemy: "We must all hang together, or we shall all hang separately."[5] Working against one another, we become weak; but working together, we become strong. By standing against the enemy as a couple, we can push forward over life's tough terrain in the Lord's strength.

Jesus said, "If a house is divided against itself, that house cannot stand" (Mark 3:25). In every marriage, conflict will come—but so can resolution. Determine to partner with your husband through the storms and through the calm. Work with him and not against him to come to an understanding. Pray for him, encourage him, help him, but don't battle him. He's not the enemy. Fight the good fight as a couple, not against each other but against anything that would destroy the unity of your marriage.

If you get angry with one another, don't stay angry. It is tempting to nurse old wounds and hold grudges. But determine instead to resolve the issue and move on. Let the matter die—so your marriage won't. As John Gottman says, "In a sense, a marriage lives and dies by what you might loosely call its arguments, by how well disagreements and grievances are aired. The key is how you argue—whether your style escalates tension or leads to a feeling of resolution."[6]

Arguments will happen, even to the best of couples. The question is, will we let them tear us apart, or will we use them to draw us closer to our husbands than ever before? Our disagreements don't need to end with a winner and a loser. Every conflict can end in win-win if we'll practice the art of positive arguing.

POWER POINT

⚙ **Read:** James 3:13–4:3. What positive marriage tools do you glean from these verses? What are some areas of personal conviction that surface from these words?

♡ **Pray:** Loving heavenly Father, beautiful Savior, thank you for rescuing me from sin and darkness. Thank you for making me a new creation. Thank you for my wonderful husband. Help us to work through our conflicts in a positive way. Unify us so that we work together against the conflict and not against each other. Bring us continually back together again in love and forgiveness. Show us when to die to self and overlook a grievance. Draw us close to you and away from the influences of the enemy. In Jesus' name I pray, amen.

💡 **Remember:** "But the wisdom that comes from heaven is first of all pure; then peace-loving, considerate, submissive, full of mercy and good fruit, impartial and sincere" (James 3:17).

☺ **Do:** On a piece of paper, write out the "Do" list from the "Rules of Engagement" section in this chapter. Look up the scripture that goes with each "do" and jot down some notes on its key points. You may want to put your paper in a plastic sleeve or frame to help you remember (and yes, memorize) these important tips for handling disagreements with dignity and grace.

Power Principle #3

THe Power OF Respect

Teach me, my God and King, in all things thee to see,
And what I do in any thing, to do it as for thee.

—George Herbert

Show proper respect to everyone: Love the brotherhood of believers, fear God, honor the king.

—1 Peter 2:17

His Secret Desire
The Gift of Respect

Respect is love in plain clothes.

—Frankie Byrne

Think back for a moment to your elementary-school years. Do you remember bringing home a prized art project that you had lovingly created in class? Most likely your mother *oohed* and *aahed* over it (never asking what it was), hugged you, then pinned the artwork on the wall or placed it under a magnet on the refrigerator. You were so proud! Mother had warmly received your work of art. She esteemed it, respected it, and gave it a place of honor.

Why did she do this? Was it because the artistic technique was so magnificent? Did your project show creative genius in the lines, colors, and textures you chose? Not quite! The plain and simple truth is that your mother loved and respected the artwork because *you* made it. It was handcrafted by the one and only you. Your mother treated it as if it were worth a million bucks, not because of the artwork itself, but in recognition of the one who created it.

Now let's take a look at the piece of work we call "The Husband." Does he have a few flaws? Is he a perfect balance of sensitivity, godliness, responsibility, and great looks? Well, probably not—but then again, neither are we. Like the artwork our mothers valued and respected because we made it, we can value and respect our husbands because God made them. They are designed and fashioned by our loving heavenly Father. Yes, God has allowed room for certain imperfections while we dwell in our sinful states here on Earth. But when we stop inspecting the creation and remind ourselves of the Creator, our whole perspective changes.

Better than Sex?

Ever since Paramount released the Mel Gibson movie *What Women Want* a couple of years ago, interest seems to have skyrocketed in finding out the "inside scoop" on what the opposite sex truly wants and desires. Perhaps you have seen some of the surveys on this topic that have been circulating in books, magazines, and e-mails. What would you guess is at the top of most husbands' lists of things they want from their wives? Sex, right? That was my first guess too. In our current cultural climate, it's easy to assume that sex dominates every man's thoughts, hopes, and dreams. And it's true that sex does rank high on most husbands' want lists. But ask men what they want first and foremost from their wives, and the majority will not say, "Sex." They'll answer, "Respect."

The apostle Paul wouldn't be surprised by that response. In one of his letters to the early Christians, Paul encouraged husbands to *love* their wives and wives to *respect* their husbands (Ephesians 5:33). In his heavenly wisdom, Paul knew what men and women really, truly want from one another. Most wives desire above all to be honestly and completely loved by their husbands. Paul recognized that men need to be reminded of that. Husbands sometimes get busy with their work or involved in their hobbies and lose their focus on loving their wives—or at least become distracted from showing it.

Since I'm not writing *The Power of a Positive Husband,* I won't try to teach husbands how to love their wives. That would have to be the subject of another book. But since I *am* writing a book for positive wives, let me ask: Why do you think Paul considered it necessary to tell wives to *respect* their husbands? Could it be that we so easily slip out of respecting our husbands and begin nitpicking and dwelling on their weaknesses? Paul delivered to wives a divine reminder: respect, respect, respect. Respect is not only what a husband wants; it's what a marriage needs. A wife who shows respect to her husband encourages her marriage to run smoothly and allows her spouse to become all that he ought to be.

Notice that Paul didn't say, "*If* a husband loves his wife, *then* the wife can respect her husband." Ephesians 5:33 is not an "if...then" proposition. Even if a husband doesn't seem to do his part, a wife must still do hers. The good news is, when one spouse does his or her part, the other spouse frequently follows. As positive wives, we shouldn't wait for our husbands to show us love before we act; we must move forward and show respect anyway. Many times a loving reaction will follow.

A beautiful example of a positive wife can be seen in First Lady Laura Bush. A woman of principle and wisdom, Laura has an obvious respect for her husband, President George W. Bush. George W. has said of his wife, "She's always asking what I'm doing about this or that, but I think she trusts me to make the right decisions."[1] Laura honors her husband with respect through the confidence and support she consistently shows him. She is a wonderful helpmate to our forty-third president and a great inspiration to the rest of us.

Respect Perspective

For most of us, respect is denoted by the kindness and reverence that we show toward another person or thing. It means we hold someone or something in high esteem. But the biblical meaning of the word goes further. Often I like to check out the Amplified version of the Bible to understand the full implication of a word or phrase. Here's how the Amplified Bible translates Ephesians 5:33: "Let the wife see that she respects *and* reverences her husband [that she notices him, regards him, honors him, prefers him, venerates and esteems him; and that she defers to him, praises him, and loves and admires him exceedingly]."

There now, that doesn't sound too hard, does it? I never suspected that so many actions could be packed into the meaning of one little word! What man wouldn't love a wife who did all this?

Let's look again at this passage and consider each phrase in light of the way we relate to our husbands. As you read the list below, substitute your name for *she* and your husband's name for *him*.

- She notices him.

- She regards him.

- She honors him.

- She prefers him.

- She venerates him.

- She esteems him.

- She defers to him.

- She praises him.

- She loves him.

- She admires him exceedingly.

How did you do? Personally, I fell a little short. My purpose in examining this verse is not to make us feel inadequate or overwhelmed, but rather to gain a well-rounded understanding of the *attitude* behind respect. It's an attitude that says we will embrace our husbands, no matter who they are or how well they stack up against our checklist of standards. It's an attitude that says we will respect our husbands unconditionally.

That's tough to do, I know. The entire ninth chapter of this book is devoted to the subject of how to show our husbands respect, even when they don't deserve it. For now, suffice it to say that just as your mother highly esteemed your school art project—not because the artwork deserved it, but because *you* made it—so, too, you should esteem and respect your husband, not because he deserves it, but because he was created by God. He is your brother in Christ and your chosen mate. Respect may not always come easily, but it is essential to having a positive and meaningful marriage.

Of course, respect must be balanced. Respecting your husband doesn't mean you worship him (as can almost be implied by the Amplified text). There is a danger in being so wrapped up in your spouse that you begin to live for him instead of for the Lord. A healthy view of respect keeps God first. Your husband can never meet all your needs; only God can. Give God the honor, reverence, and respect due his name; and give your husband respect out of obedience to God.

A Tough Word

When Paul wrote Ephesians 5:33, he was actually capping off a discussion he'd begun earlier in his letter. To better understand this scripture, we need to venture back several verses and get the broader context in view. Warning: These verses contain a word that may seem offensive to women. In light of today's culture and the modern push for women's equality, this word is what I would call countercultural, to say the least. For this reason, I want to preface what you are about to read by affirming that Jesus was a great liberator of women. In Jewish society in Jesus' day, women were regarded as lowly and insignificant. Jesus brought them up to a higher status and introduced them to a place of honor.

Each one of you also must love his wife as he loves himself; and the wife must respect her husband. —Ephesians 5:33

103

Women played significant roles in his ministry and in the early church. They were highly regarded by Paul and Peter as well.

As you read these words of Paul, then, understand that he is not commenting on a woman's worth; he is providing working principles for a marriage: "Submit to one another out of reverence for Christ. Wives, submit to your husbands as to the Lord. For the husband is the head of the wife as Christ is the head of the church, his body, of which he is the Savior. Now as the church submits to Christ, so also wives should submit to their husbands in everything" (Ephesians 5:21–24).

There it is: the S word. *Submit.* But don't jump to conclusions too quickly. Have you ever looked at a piece of art in a museum and thought to yourself, *How pitiful! That's not art—that's junk?* You might have had a different perspective, however, if you could have heard the artist's explanation of the work and understood the meaning behind it. In the same way, you might have a different feeling about the word *submit* once you hear the heart and understand the intent of the one who wrote it.

Often we have negative reactions to the idea of submission because we haven't grasped its full meaning. We may have difficulty submitting to authority in general, especially God's authority. But submission is a common part of life. It's a continual part of relating to others. Think for a moment about the many life circumstances in which we submit. In school a student submits to the teacher's authority. Citizens submit to the laws of the land. In friendships we submit back and forth to one another's interests. As Christians we continually submit to God's authority.

The original Greek word translated *submit* in Ephesians 5:21–22 is *hupotasso,* meaning "subject" or "subjection." It is primarily a military term, as when a soldier ranks under a superior officer and willingly yields his or her rights. That functional order is critical to the success of any army. It's just as critical to the success of any marriage.

In marriage we are not independent of our spouses; we're *inter*dependent. We're a team, working toward a common goal. The question is, what's the best way for two people of equal worth but different strengths, skills, and attributes to get something done? The answer is submission. When we willingly submit to our husbands' leadership, we are able to work more effectively to fulfill God's plans for our lives together.

This authority structure is not meant to be a chain around our necks, but a loving, protective covering given to us by God. As Christ is the head of the church, so our husbands have the headship in the home—and along with that, a great responsibility before God to lead their families in a godly way. And just as the church submits to the love and authority of Christ, so we as wives are called to submit to the love and authority of our husbands.

That doesn't mean we become their doormats. Nor does it mean we remain silent when we have opinions or ideas. Quite the contrary; marriage is a working together, a complementing of one another's gifts and abilities. In a godly marriage, a wife's thoughts and opinions are to be as highly valued as her husband's. We would be missing Paul's point if we thought a submissive wife should never disagree with her husband or a husband should never yield to his wife. In the Garden of Eden, Eve was given to Adam as a complement and a helper—not a subservient being. She was formed from a rib taken from his side, not a bone scraped from the bottom of his foot.

It's not often that couples find themselves at a point of decision that requires the "higher-ranking" spouse to make the final call. When this happens, the husband does have the final authority—but he also has the weight of responsibility before God for making the best decision for his family. As positive wives, we must be willing to submit in such instances.

But while these actual acts of submission are rare, the underlying attitude of respecting our husbands' leadership ought to be continual. Submission is really all about choosing to respect our husbands in their God-given role. A consistently respectful attitude is a fragrant aroma that can soothe a marriage as it permeates the home.

The Gift

Recently I took great pleasure in reading *Zig,* the autobiography of Zig Ziglar. In this colorful life story of a truly positive man, I also saw the image of a profoundly positive wife. Zig affectionately refers to her as "the Redhead." Through the early years of financial struggles and job changes, the Ziglars moved many times. This would be enough to exasperate most wives, but not the Redhead. She continued to love, honor, and respect Zig through the lean years. In his book Zig mentions many times how blessed he was to have a wife who always supported and believed in him.[2]

There is possibly no greater gift we can give our husbands than the gift of respect. Yes, respect is a gift. No strings attached. No "if...then" lists. Respect is wrapped up in the beautiful paper of kind and gentle words and tied with the enormous ribbon of a loving spirit. It is a pouring out of ourselves. It's going beyond what we want and offering our husbands what they need. It is not an easy gift to give.

But then the greatest blessings in life are rarely free. They come with a hefty price tag, because they are of great value. I think of Gretchen who invested many long hours of research, development, and hard work to start a jewelry business. It wasn't easy, but owning and operating her own business had always been her dream. The end result, she will tell you, has been worth the sacrifice.

I think of Patti who, along with her husband, built her dream house. The couple put in many hours of planning, shopping, and poring over carpet samples and paint chips. They willingly made the effort because the house had great value to them. The end result is a wonderful home they can now enjoy with family and friends.

Marriage is a valuable asset that requires an investment of self-sacrifice and respect from both husband and wife. But whether or not our husbands do their part, as positive wives we must do ours. We must extend the gift of respect and honor to our husbands, helping them to become the men God created them to be. Yes, respect is a gift with no strings attached. But we do receive something in return: the blessing of husbands who are enabled to reach their potential and become the men God intended. Our respect is a catalyst that moves our husbands toward greatness. You've heard it said, "Behind every great man stands a great woman." How true! A husband's greatness flows from the respect and honor his wife gives him.

In Proverbs 31 we read about the characteristics of a noble wife. Verse 23 tells us, "Her husband is respected at the city gate, where he takes his seat among the elders of the land." Why do you think this woman's husband is respected at the city gate (the place where court was held in biblical times)? I think it's because his wife gives him the gift of respect at home. Her respect is the catalyst that enables him to move out into the community with confidence and integrity and gain the respect of others.

As positive wives we need to understand that respect is a powerful tool in our hands. What happens when a wife respects her husband? He moves forward, knowing that the person who is closest to him in all the world sees his potential and backs him up. It's a powerful thing to have someone support you and believe in you. Think about the people in your life who've believed in you, who've encouraged you to use your gifts and talents and pursue your dreams. Isn't it wonderful to be able to pass on that same kind of support to your husband?

What happens when a wife withholds respect from her husband? He becomes discouraged. He loses the motivation to move forward. A nagging wife at his back slows him down and brings him down. After all, if his own wife doesn't respect him, what are the chances he will respect himself? She becomes "like decay in his bones," as Proverbs 12:4 says. May it never be so in our homes!

What does disrespect look like? Consider the following list:

- Frowning
- Rolling your eyes
- Giving verbal put downs or snubs
- Arguing constantly
- Making snide comments that insinuate he is not a good provider or spiritual leader
- Lying to him
- Making sex conditional
- Putting him down in front of his friends or yours
- Disregarding the guidelines he sets up with you for the family finances
- Ignoring him

What does respect look like? It shows itself in these ways:

- Smiling at him
- Embracing or hugging him when he comes home
- Giving him a vote of confidence
- Writing him a note of encouragement
- Looking at him with a sparkle in your eyes that says, "After all these years, I still think you're the greatest!"

- Bragging on him in front of others
- Admiring his abilities
- Abiding by the financial guidelines you've agreed upon
- Paying attention to him
- Listening to him
- Cooking his favorite dinner
- Encouraging him to reach his goals and follow his dreams
- Allowing him space to pursue his hobbies
- Encouraging his (good) guy friendships
- Building him up and supporting him in front of the kids

The list could go on, but you get the idea!

Visit to an Art Gallery

Curt and I recently celebrated our twentieth anniversary with a trip to California. One of our favorite things to do when we travel is to visit the local art galleries, so we stopped in a gallery that happened to have on display several original sketches by Rembrandt and Matisse. The drawings were rough and not really much to look at, but oh, were they valuable! Based on their price tags, I can assure you, they were held in high esteem. Why? Because they were from the hands of two of the world's most renowned artists. Once again I was reminded that it's not the artwork itself but the artist who makes a work of art valuable.

Our husbands are unique creations of God. As positive wives let us look at them with respect—as if we were standing before a drawing by a great artist. Maybe your husband is still a work in progress. (Aren't we all?) That doesn't matter; he is valuable because of the one who made him. Notice him. Honor him. Prefer him. Esteem him. Remember that he has come to you from the hand of your wonderful heavenly Father, the greatest artist of all.

POWER POINT

⚙ **Read:** 2 Samuel 6:12–23. Here we have the unfortunate picture of disrespect in a marriage, demonstrating how very important respect is to a husband. What did David do that his wife Michal didn't approve of? How did she show him disrespect? How did David feel about her lack of respect? What were the consequences?

♡ **Pray:** Glorious Lord and Savior, thank you for the wonderful covering you have placed over us as wives. Thank you for my husband. Help me to give him the gift of respect all of the days of our marriage. May my submission to him reflect the submission of the church to Christ. Teach me new and creative ways to show respect to my husband, and use that respect to build him up and encourage him to pursue your calling in his life. Work in his life and mine, allowing us to become all we've been created to be for your glory. In Jesus' name I pray, amen.

💡 **Remember:** "Each one of you also must love his wife as he loves himself, and the wife must respect her husband" (Ephesians 5:33).

☺ **Do:** Take time to be alone before God and reflect on your relationship with your husband. As you submit to God's leadership, ask him to reveal to you any ways in which you show your husband disrespect. Pray for God to help you respect and esteem your husband in those particular areas. Look for several opportunities this week to say or do something to show your husband that you respect him.

Attitude Is Everything
Building a Better Marriage with a Brighter Outlook

*The greater part of our happiness or misery depends
on our dispositions, and not our circumstances.*

—Martha Washington

Recently our family visited a delightful inn that was perfectly positioned on a quiet lake in the foothills of the Smokey Mountains. Greystone Inn is one of the happiest places I have ever visited. Why? I believe the reason traces back to the owners of the inn, Tim and Boo Boo (yes, her name is Boo Boo) Lovelace. On any given day you can find this upbeat couple chatting with their guests during afternoon tea on the front porch. As dusk approaches, Tim likes to take the guests on a sunset cruise around the lake in his electric-powered boat. Tim and Boo Boo enjoy what they do; but more importantly, they love life and love the people in their lives.

This attitude seems to trickle down to the manager and bellman of the inn. They greet the guests with warmth, respect, and a "what-can-I-do-to-make-your-stay-wonderful?" type of spirit. From there the positive outlook spills over to the wait staff, who smile and chat with the guests and offer to help beyond the call of duty. Our stay was delightful because we were surrounded by kindness and affirmation the entire week. We even found ourselves encouraging and serving one another more within our family. The uplifting attitude was contagious!

A positive attitude has a powerful effect on the people around us. Perhaps you are thinking, *But I don't feel like being positive and perky all the time.* Having a positive attitude doesn't mean that we deny our feelings and overlook hurts. There is "a time to weep and a time to laugh," as Ecclesiastes 3:4 says. We should never negate our emotions; but in the midst of experiencing them, our attitude *can* remain constant. A positive attitude is not a feeling but an underlying outlook we have toward people and toward life. It represents a hope and faith that is rooted within our hearts.

The Scent of a Woman

Have you ever heard it said that some people brighten a room just by their presence, while others brighten the room by leaving? We want to be room lighters, not gloomy grumblers. Jesus told his followers, "Let your light shine before men, that they may see your good deeds and praise your Father in heaven" (Matthew 5:16). He wasn't saying we should be Sally Smiles or Frieda Fake or Polly Perfect; he was saying that God has placed his gospel of truth, joy, and hope in our hearts, and we shouldn't hide it. We should let it radiate from our lives. And as we shine with the Lord's love, others will be drawn to him.

One of my favorite authors is Robert Louis Stevenson. A gifted and prolific writer as an adult, he was often ill as a child. Because he so easily caught cold from the brisk winter winds in his hometown of Edinburgh, Scotland, his parents kept him inside all season long. All that he saw of the world in those months was through his nursery window. Many of his childhood days were spent in bed, but little Robert made the best of his plight by playing with his toy ships and toy soldiers and building imaginary cities on what he called "the pleasant land of counterpane." His reflections on this time were the basis for his poem, "The Land of Counterpane":

When I was sick and lay a-bed,

I had two pillows at my head,

And all my toys beside me lay

To keep me happy all the day.

And sometimes for an hour or so

I watched my leaden soldiers go,

With different uniforms and drills,

Among the bed-clothes, through the hills;

And sometimes sent my ships in fleets

All up and down among the sheets;

Or brought my trees and houses out,

And planted cities all about.

I was the giant great and still

That sits upon the pillow-hill,

And sees before him, dale and plain,

The pleasant land of counterpane.[1]

Although he could have nursed a sour attitude in life due to his physical restrictions, Stevenson chose to view the world in a bright and positive way. He learned to make the best of his situation. Where did this attitude get its roots? From the two women in Stevenson's childhood who greatly influenced his outlook on life. One was his mother— "my jewelest of mothers," he called her—who made his dull nursery a sunshiny, happy place. Although she was not physically strong herself, she was always ready to play in the nursery with her young son. The other woman was his nurse, Alison Cunningham—"Cummie" to little Robert—who was patient and gentle and always there to drive away his fears and soothe his pain.

In the springtime Robert was no longer confined to his nursery, and he spent much of his time in his grandfather's garden. "Like the flowers, he began to lift up his head and grow strong in the sunshine," wrote one of his biographers. "It was a different world to him when the sun shone and the sky was blue, and the splendid colors of the flowers made his days a rainbow riot of delight."[2]

The story is told that later in his life, when he was suffering with tuberculosis, his wife heard him hacking and coughing and came into his room. "I suppose you still believe it is a wonderful day," she commented negatively. Stevenson turned toward his window, which was ablaze with sunlight, and responded, "I do! I will never let a row of medicine bottles block my horizon."[3]

Stevenson maintained his positive attitude throughout the difficult times of his life. Life happens, and it is not always pleasant. But whatever our ups and downs, one thing *can* remain constant: the outlook we choose to have in life. We have the power to influence and color the situations of our lives by our attitudes. Will we choose to see the world in hopeful hues of vibrant color or will we choose to paint our challenges in gloomy, doomy gray? The choice is ours as it was for Robert Louis Stevenson. How sad to think that his wife did not make the positive choice he did.

No "If Onlys"

Perhaps you are wondering what a positive attitude has to do with respecting our husbands. Respect involves positive choices. We must choose to speak kindly about our spouses and not tear them down behind their backs. We must choose to see and honor their good qualities while choosing to overlook some of their faults. We must choose to build our homes with respect and not tear them down with contention—and that process begins with our choice of attitude. I'm reminded of Solomon's words in Proverbs 14:1: "The wise woman builds her house, but with her own hands the foolish one tears hers down." Whether we're home builders or home destroyers depends on the attitude of our hearts and the outlook we choose.

Many wives waste away their lives with the "if-only" disease: "If only my husband worked harder." "If only my husband were the spiritual leader in our home." "If only he were more sensitive to my feelings." "If only he spent more time with me." "If only _____." (You fill in the blank.) We all have things we wish were different in our lives, in our marriages, and especially with our spouses. But the if-only disease only serves to eat us up inside and fosters an angry disrespect for our husbands. We must choose daily not to give in to it.

In a recent "Dear Abby" column, several letters were sent in to comment on the old adage "If *ifs* and *ands* were pots and pans, there'd be no work for tinkers." One wise woman who wrote in explained her philosophy on attitude. She said:

> Not only do I remember my mother quoting the same phrase to me, she had another one: "If wishes were horses, beggars would ride." Both are from a bygone generation that held no truck with the "If only" and "I wish" mentality. In other words, if you want something to happen in your life, work for it. If something happens you don't like, deal with it, grow from it, and move on. Don't just wish, complain, and blame. We could use a little more of that sage wisdom in this day of frivolous lawsuits, cheating in schools and business, etc.[4]

We could add to her list the divorces caused by blame and disrespect. The if-only disease is rampant in our blame-it-on-someone-else society. But Scripture gives us a prescription for preventing this disease from settling in our hearts and minds and destroying our marriages.

Better to live in a desert than with a quarrelsome and ill-tempered wife. —Proverbs 21:19

Power Principle #3: The Power of Respect

It is found in Philippians 4:4–9. Warning: This is powerful stuff! Ingest daily until it becomes a part of your life.

> Rejoice in the Lord always. I will say it again: Rejoice! Let your gentleness be evident to all. The Lord is near. Do not be anxious about anything, but in everything, by prayer and petition, with thanksgiving, present your requests to God. And the peace of God, which transcends all understanding, will guard your hearts and your minds in Christ Jesus.
>
> Finally, brothers, whatever is true, whatever is noble, whatever is right, whatever is pure, whatever is lovely, whatever is admirable—if anything is excellent or praiseworthy—think about such things. Whatever you have learned or received or heard from me, or seen in me—put it into practice. And the God of peace will be with you.

Wow! There's some medicine we could all use at times, however difficult it may be to swallow. I confess I need it. The if-only disease manifests itself in my life when I think, *If only Curt would put his arm around me in church, then I'd know that he really loves me.* How ridiculous! Curt isn't a huggy type of guy. I know that. Just because he doesn't put his arm around me doesn't mean he doesn't love me. *Get over it and grow up, Karol!* I have to tell myself. *Focus on what Curt does do to show his love and esteem.*

Or I think, *If only we didn't live in Dallas, where all the women are so beautiful because of their expensive clothes and contoured bodies (thanks to plastic surgery).* Again I have to tell myself, *Deal with it, Karol! Quit looking at what other people have or what they've had done, and keep your focus on truth.* And what's the truth? That anywhere I live, I will find lovely people and not-so-lovely people. That there is much more to life than striving for riches or beauty. That the important thing is to develop lasting and beautiful qualities in the hidden person of the heart. Sometimes a strong dose of Philippians 4:4–9 is just what the doctor ordered to soothe the destructive attitude of wishes, wants, and if onlys!

Blessings Inventory

When is the last time you reflected on the blessings you have experienced? God is at work in our lives each day, but we often forget to take stock of the good he is doing. We easily notice things we don't like or things we wish were different; but how rarely we ponder the good that arrives daily on our doorsteps!

In their profound book *The Generosity Factor,* Ken Blanchard and S. Truett Cathy recommend taking a "blessings inventory."[5] By making a list that recognizes the good things that take place in your life each day, as well as what has been good throughout your lifetime, your attitude and your outlook are transformed. Your eyes are opened to the good and lovely things in your life. Start your list by naming the people who are or who have been a blessing to you. Once you get started, your thoughts will begin to flow, and your list will grow longer. More importantly, your heart will begin to fill up with gratitude. During difficult or challenging circumstances, this exercise can help you keep things in perspective.

The blessings inventory idea was beautifully portrayed in the lives of Martin and Gracia Burnham, American missionaries in the Philippines who were captured by the Abu Sayaf Guerillas (ASG) in 2001. During their dramatic rescue from captivity in the spring of 2002, Martin was caught in the crossfire and killed. But his life and Gracia's are a testimony to the power and beauty of a positive attitude and a thankful perspective. During their time as prisoners, Martin graciously offered to carry things for their captors as well as for the other hostages. Every night, as Martin was chained to a tree by an ASG guard, he would thank the guard and wish him a good night. According to Gracia, Martin was highly respected by all of their ASG captors because he so consistently displayed the love and compassion of Christ.

One day, after a long and tiring hike with the ASG, the Burnhams strung up a hammock and sat down to talk together. Martin reflected, "It's been a very hard year, but it has also been a very good year." Then they began to thank the Lord for everything they could think of, starting with their hammock and their boots. They went on to thank God for all the believers they had ever met, and God encouraged their hearts with the remembrance of each person, couple, family, and church that they knew was praying for them.

Psalm 100:2 often came to Martin's mind: "Worship the LORD with gladness; come before him with joyful songs." "We might not leave this jungle alive," Martin said, "but at least we can leave this world serving the Lord with *gladness*. We can serve him right here where we are, and with gladness."

Just before Martin passed from this world to his heavenly home, the Burnhams prayed together, thanked God for his faithfulness, and then lay down for a nap. They were awakened by gunfire exchanged between the ASG and a group of Philippine scout rangers who had come to rescue the hostages. Martin was hit and ushered into the presence of his loving Lord.

Being held hostage didn't keep the Burnhams from thanking God, praising him, and reflecting on his blessings. Keeping a blessings inventory not only gave them strength, it built their faith and the faith of those around them.[6] If the Burnhams could thank God in the midst of their primitive captivity in the Philippine jungle, surely we can live thankful lives in the comfort and safety of our own homes!

The Choice Is Ours

We have a tendency to make our attitudes dependent upon our circumstances. But if we wait until we "feel like it," a positive attitude may never happen. No, our attitude is a choice we must make each day. Will I focus on what is wrong in my life, or will I choose to see what God can do in and through my circumstances? I'm thankful that Paul chose to wear the bright glasses of hope in the midst of his circumstances. He found himself in a prison cell on numerous occasions for simply preaching about Jesus. He had the perfect justification for crying, "No fair!" "It's 'no fair' that I'm in this prison cell! It is 'no fair' that God would let me be here when I was only doing his will!"

When is the last time you cried, "No fair"? Perhaps you said it because you were comparing your situation with someone else's. "It's 'no fair' that her husband is kind and sensitive, while mine is oblivious to my feelings." "It's 'no fair' that my husband works late all the time and other husbands don't." "It's 'no fair' that _____." (You fill in the blank.)

It would have been easy for Paul to look at his circumstances, stop dead in his tracks, and give up his work. But instead of seeing his prison cell as a dead end, he saw it as an opportunity to spread hope. He ministered to prisoners and prison guards. He wrote letters to the early Christian churches and to his fellow laborers in Christ. These letters were messages of hope and encouragement. In fact, the words we read earlier from Philippians 4 were written while Paul was a prisoner: "Rejoice in the Lord always...."

Paul spoke of being content in every circumstance. He went on to pen one of the greatest statements of hope ever uttered: "I can do all things through Christ who strengthens me" (Philippians 4:13 NKJV). You have probably heard this phrase used as a motivational tool many times, but did you know that Paul was talking about being content?

Paul's key to contentment and a positive outlook was simple: Recognize that you can make it through any circumstance through the strength that Christ alone can give.

Do you find your strength in Christ? Do you lean on him for help through thick and thin? What circumstances are you struggling with right now—and are you depending on Jesus to help you in the midst of them?

Again, I'm not saying we ought to be smiley and happy in difficult situations. There is a time for mourning and grief. Yet, even in the midst of the grief, we can maintain a glimmer of hope. A hope in God. A hope that God will not leave us but will be with us, even through the valley of the shadow of death.

Our hope is not in ourselves or other people or better circumstances. Our hope is in a redeeming God who can take a dead relationship and make it vibrant once again. He can take a broken life and make it whole. Just as surely as God raised Jesus from the dead, so our loving heavenly Father can resurrect a lifeless situation—including a lifeless marriage. He may not act in the way we think he should or want him to. But then again, he is our Creator and our friend, and we can rest assured that he always acts in our best interest—even when we don't know what our best interest is.

Ultimately, a positive outlook comes not from outside circumstances but from the position of our hearts. It comes from a sure faith in God's loving sovereignty. The choice is ours. Will we wallow in despair, or will we be hopeful in expectation?

Attitude and the Act of Respect

Several years ago I asked Curt what he needed most when he came home in the evenings from a work-weary day. Was it a clean house? (I hoped it wasn't.) Was it dinner on the table? (I could do that, if he didn't insist that every meal be home cooked.) Curt pondered his answer carefully. I think he knew that I wouldn't be asking again for a while! Finally he said, "Karol, what I really need when I come home in the evenings is for you to greet me with an upbeat attitude and a smile."

My first thought was, *Crumb! I thought the haggard, worn-out look was a good strategy.* I had figured that by showing him how difficult my day had been, he would be kinder and more sensitive to my feelings. But the truth was, that strategy had never really been effective. So I decided to go ahead and comply with his request.

Now understand, we have two giant dogs in our home. One is an overweight golden retriever named Honey, and one is a white Great Pyrenees named Bear. Whenever we come through the door, Bear makes it a policy to run and greet us with a big "Bear hug." And I mean *big.* When Bear puts his paws on my shoulders, his head towers over mine. Trust me, we have to be ready for the greeting, or he will knock us over.

I made it my goal to beat Bear to the door when Curt came home in the evenings. That's still my goal. I'm a fast runner, but I always lose. We end up having one big group hug at the door. Bear wags his tail, and I give Curt the gift of a smile and a kind word to let him know I'm glad he's home. Do I feel like smiling every time? Honestly, no. But I have learned that a smile doesn't have to be based on feelings. When I think of it as a gift I can give to others, I see a smile in a different light. It all goes back to that old principle "It's not all about me."

A smile is a wonderful way to uplift people and give them a brighter day. It's also a wonderful way to lift our own attitudes. Try giving the gift of a smile to your husband and the other people around you for an entire day, and see how it makes you feel inside. When you give away a smile and give a lift to others, you can't help but feel good yourself. Remember, actions first; feelings follow!

I noticed that when I began respecting Curt's wish for a warm greeting and a smile, he started becoming a little more upbeat too. Over time the atmosphere of our home became more positive. Curt began coming home earlier (not necessarily the result I was hoping for, since I had lots of things I wanted to get done before he came home; still, I was always glad to see him). The moral of the story is, when we give joy to others, it tends to come back to us in greater measure.

Atmospheric Conditions

As wives we are the tone-setters for our homes. Our influence is powerful. Just as we can buy different fragrances to add a scent to the air in our homes, so we can choose different attitudes to create an aroma in the atmosphere. Which one of the following "air fresheners" do you use most often?

- Cheery and Joyful

- Grumbling and Whining

- Continually Content

- Complaining and Argumentative

- Hopeful and Happy

- Discouraged and Discontented

Ruth Bell Graham is one woman who chose long ago to create a positive atmosphere in her home. The wife of renowned evangelist Billy Graham, Ruth could have chosen to grumble and complain about her husband's job, which caused him to be away from home often. But she chose a different attitude—one that supported her husband and his ministry. Her life was not without pain and loneliness, but she chose to take that hurt to God instead of letting it linger.

There were many times she could have dallied in discontentment. For example, when she dropped off her youngest son, Ned, at school in England and returned to an empty house in North Carolina, she could have been consumed with loneliness and self-pity. The empty-nest syndrome is hard to overcome. But here's what she said about that time:

> I dreaded returning to that now empty house. But as I entered the front door and looked down the length of the hall and up the steps leading to the children's now vacant rooms, suddenly it wasn't empty. I was greeted by a living Presence, and I realized anew how true His last words were: "Lo, I am with you" (Matthew 28:20). I was surrounded by loving memories and the comfortableness of knowing I was home. This was my base of operations.[7]

America's great news commentator Paul Harvey had this to say about Billy and Ruth Graham: "I used to worry about Billy. When he started out, there was all that adulation. I was worried he might be tilted off balance by it. But then I met Ruth. Then I relaxed, knowing he had that strength on which to lean."[8] What a high compliment to a positive wife! We can only speculate this side of heaven on the eternal impact her love and support for Billy have had in this world. By her encouraging respect for him and his calling, she allowed Billy the freedom to be who he was created to be: one of the greatest preachers this world has ever known.

Life circumstances weren't always easy for the Grahams, and Ruth freely speaks of the challenges in her books (she has written nine) and through her poetry. I close now with one of her poems. It reveals so beautifully her choice to live positively through the storms of life.

We live a time secure;

Sure

It cannot last

For long

Then

The good-byes come

Again, again

Like a small death,

The closing of a door.

One learns to live

With pain.

One looks ahead,

Not back,

…never back,

only before.

And joy will come again

Warm and secure,

If only for the now,

Laughing

We endure.[9]

POWER POINT

Read: Proverbs 19:13; 21:9, 19; 25:24; 27:15. How would you describe the woman in these verses from Proverbs? How is she choosing to destroy her home? Why do you think Solomon repeated the same descriptive phrase so often? What choices can you make to become a crown to your husband and not decay to his bones?

Pray: Wonderful Lord, I praise you, for you are a redeeming God. Thank you for taking this world full of sin, sorrow, and despair and bringing forgiveness, healing, and hope. You are my rock and my refuge, and I place my trust in you. Turn my eyes toward you when I begin to worry. Turn my heart toward you when I am discouraged. Help me to be content in the circumstances I cannot change, relying always in Christ's strength. May my attitude reflect my faith in your redemptive power. In Jesus' name I pray, amen.

Remember: "Rejoice in the Lord always. I will say it again: Rejoice!" (Philippians 4:4).

Do: Choose one day this week to ban worry, grumbling, and whining from your heart, mind, and mouth. Replace those bad habits with thankfulness, joy, prayer, and hope. You may want to place reminder notes around the house to keep you looking up all day instead of down. Practice smiling, and determine to give your husband the gift of your smile when he arrives home from work.

What If He Doesn't Deserve It?
Right Responses When He Is Wrong

*Weather the storms of life by turning toward one another
and building into each other rather than rejecting one another.*

—Dennis and Barbara Rainey

Respect. It's easy to give to those who deserve it. But what if your husband doesn't deserve it? Maybe he makes the same financial blunders over and over again. Perhaps he is consistently lazy or deceitful or rude. It could be that he has broken your trust in some form or fashion or maybe even broken the law.

Many women find themselves struggling to respect their husbands, because quite frankly, their husbands haven't earned their respect. And that makes sense. If we blindly respect our husbands, aren't we letting them off the hook and giving them a green light to do whatever they want? Then again, if we respect our husbands only when they have earned it, doesn't that put them on a performance-based roller coaster?

Respect is a complicated issue when you're dealing with imperfect people. In this chapter we are going to wrestle with tough questions that arise from not-so-simple situations and discover biblical truths we can apply to them. As positive women we must find practical ways to respect our husbands—even when it's a challenge to do so.

127

Who Deserves It?

Let's be honest. Our husbands may have glaring faults, but we are not without fault ourselves. We all struggle in certain areas. Each of us has qualities that are wonderfully deserving of respect, but we also have a few disgraceful qualities that we wish no one would notice. We are all imperfect and sinful. Certainly, some areas of weakness are more obvious and intrusive than others; but the point is, none of us *deserve* forgiveness or respect.

That's where grace comes in. God's grace toward us looks past our sin and unconditionally loves us through Christ. This wonderful grace and unmerited favor is spelled out in one of my favorite passages in the Bible, Romans 5:6–8: "For while we were still helpless, at the right time Christ died for the ungodly. For one will hardly die for a righteous man; though perhaps for the good man someone would dare even to die. But God demonstrates His own love toward us, in that while we were yet sinners, Christ died for us" (NASB).

As I read those words, I am amazed once again at the wonder of the grace of God. To think that a perfect, loving God would care for sinful men and women—enough to send his own Son to die on our behalf! I'm eternally grateful that we do not have to earn our salvation. God's grace is given freely. As it says in Ephesians 2:8–9, "For it is by grace you have been saved, through faith—and this not from yourselves, it is the gift of God—not by works, so that no one can boast." The question is, if God so freely lavishes his grace on us, should we not also lavish grace on others, especially our beloved (or supposedly loved) spouses?

Yes, your husband can be wrong. I don't need to know your specific situation to know that your husband has faults, sins, and flaws; but respect is not something you give because it's deserved. It's a gift of grace, and you and I need grace just as much as our husbands do. As we learned in chapter 7, we can revere and love our husbands simply because they are unique and valued creations of God, specially given to us in marriage.

Why do we need to respect our husbands? The bottom line answer is this: Scripture tells us to. Ephesians 5:33 says that "the wife must respect her husband." Respect is not so much an act of obedience to our husbands as it is an act of obedience to God. There are no conditions applied to this command. God simply tells us to do it. Yes, people can earn our respect and approval by their good behavior or praiseworthy actions. But that doesn't mean we have the right to disobey God by denying respect to those who don't earn it.

Perhaps you're thinking, *I'm sorry, but I just can't respect my husband. It's impossible.* And on human terms, you're right. But reflect with me for a moment on the words of 2 Peter 1:3: "His divine power has given us everything we need for life and godliness." You are not on your own. You have the power of the Holy Spirit at work in your life, helping you to respect your husband even when it doesn't seem logical.

I wish we all showed unconditional love and respect to one another, but the truth is, those qualities only come perfectly from God. It's only as we allow God's love and grace to flow through us that we can begin to reflect the unconditional love and respect for our spouses that he desires.

Tough Love, Tough Respect, Tough Line

In their book *Fit to Be Tied,* Bill and Lynne Hybels speak of the importance of maintaining respect for one another, even when it's not easy. They write: "Relationships can weather thunderstorms and gale-force winds as long as there is one very important element present: respect."[1]

But doesn't respecting our spouses unconditionally mean that we're approving of their actions? That's a valid question. There is a justifiable tension between approval and respect. Can we regard, honor, and esteem our husbands while we're disapproving of their behavior? Absolutely. It may be difficult to do both, but it's not impossible. And in fact, respect and disapproval can work together quite well. We can have a positive, powerful impact on our husbands by showing them respect as persons, even as we make perfectly clear that we don't endorse what they're doing.

Respecting a husband's personhood means acknowledging his free will (just as God acknowledges ours) and recognizing that he has the freedom to make wrong choices. If a husband continues to make choices that are hurtful and destructive to the foundation of trust in marriage, a wife may need to consider what boundaries she will draw out of self-respect and respect for the marriage itself. Even then she can show respect for her husband's personhood by making herself available to listen to his concerns, supporting his friendships with godly men who come alongside to help him, and encouraging him to confront the issues underlying his bad choices.

Case in point: Tami is disgusted with her husband, Brian. He has been out of work for six months, and the family finances are dwindling quickly. Tami's paycheck as an executive assistant barely covers the monthly bills and leaves no room for savings, clothing, or vacations. Meanwhile, Brian watches television, reads the newspaper, and does very little to help around the house while he waits for the "right job" to materialize that will "best utilize his skills and talents." When Tami comes home in the evenings after fighting through rush-hour traffic, she wants to scream at Brian, "Get off the couch and get a job! I don't care if you work at Burger King. Just do something productive!"

How can Tami handle this situation in a positive way? How can she show respect to Brian while letting him know she doesn't approve of his activity (or should we say, *inactivity*)? She can demonstrate respect through the kindness of her words and actions. She can speak to Brian in a kind, gentle voice. She can look at him with love, not disgust. She can show respect by *not* stomping into the house, slamming the door, glaring at Brian, or yelling at him (all of which would be tempting to do). Tami can respect her husband by guarding her mouth with her friends and coworkers and not talking about him behind his back in a demeaning way.

She can esteem him yet respectfully disagree with his actions by means of healthy discussion, not nagging. Tami can listen to Brian's point of view and thereby honor him, but she can also respectfully offer her point of view. Understanding that he doesn't want his gifts and talents wasted, she can help him brainstorm all the job possibilities. She can work with him to create a logical plan of action that includes a designated time period. (For example, if Brian has not found a permanent job within a month, he will begin looking for an interim job to help with the finances.) Tami can also tell Brian that she would appreciate some help around the house while she is working and he's at home.

By joining together with Brian instead of against him, Tami can best encourage him to become a better person. As his teammate, she is in the perfect position to help him overcome his weaknesses and move forward with his life. Like all of us, though, she must guard against two temptations:

1. The Desire to Control

Often we want to force an outcome and make the end result come about in our own way. We must learn to work together with our husbands without controlling or nagging, coming alongside them as their companions, not their drill sergeants.

2. The Tendency to Enable

Sometimes we try to cover for our husbands when they are caught in a rut—but all that does is help them stay in the rut! Instead, we must

To do what is right and just is more acceptable to the LORD than sacrifice. —Proverbs 21:3

carefully help them out of the pit they're in and encourage them to pursue a more positive, healthy lifestyle. This can be a delicate process and may require help from wise and godly mentors or counselors.

(Side note: Some situations or behaviors are dangerous or unlawful. In such cases, it is vital to seek help. Pornography, extramarital affairs, alcohol or drug abuse, violence—these are serious matters that should not be taken lightly. If your husband struggles with one or more of these issues, prayerfully work through a plan of confrontation and intervention with godly counselors and close friends by your side.)

In Tami and Brian's case, imagine what would happen if Tami chose not to respect her husband but rather to vent her disapproval through the venue of disrespect. Not a pretty picture! Her degrading words and angry tone would probably zap every ounce of confidence and self-respect that Brian has (and that certainly wouldn't help his job search). I'm not saying that showing respect is easy to do in a situation like Tami's. She absolutely needs God's strength and self-control working through her to accomplish it. But by choosing the way of respect, she can help build Brian's self-esteem and confidence. By giving him honor, she can encourage him to recognize his place as head of the home and motivate him to assume that responsibility.

Two Boats

A dear friend of mine—I'll call her Sharon—struggled through a difficult marriage for almost twenty years. She found herself arguing with her husband all the time, trying to change his misguided ways. Then, through godly counsel from wise friends (very important in the struggle to respect), she began to seek God's will and his Word. And to her surprise, she—not her husband—began to change.

Sharon says she was impacted in particular by two boat stories from the Bible. You may be familiar with them. The first one tells the story of Peter stepping out of a fishing boat and walking on the water toward Jesus. You can read it in detail in Matthew 14:28–33. As Peter walked toward the Lord, he began to focus on the raging waves around him, and he started to sink. "Lord, save me!" he cried out. Immediately Jesus reached out his hand and caught Peter, saying, "You of little faith, why did you doubt?"

Sharon says that when she read this story, she realized that she was a lot like Peter in her marriage. Her eyes were constantly on all the wrong things—her husband's mistakes and shortcomings—instead of on the Lord. When she began to take her eyes off her husband's imperfections and put them on a perfect God who is able to help her through seemingly impossible circumstances, her perspective—and her marriage—started to change.

The second boat story is found in Matthew 8:23–27. The disciples were in a boat and Jesus was asleep in the bow when a furious storm blew in. As the waves swept over the boat, the disciples feared for their lives. "Lord, save us! We're going to drown!" they cried. Once again Jesus spoke a simple phrase: "You of little faith, why are you so afraid?" Then he rebuked the wind and the waves, and the lake became perfectly calm.

Sharon admits that she often felt panicked and worried about her husband's problems, thinking they would overwhelm her (like the waves in the story). But then she realized that Jesus was in the boat—and her marriage—with her. He had never left her; she had simply forgotten that he was there, ready and able to do the impossible. The story underscored what she had already learned: She must get her focus off the waves (her husband's problems) and onto the Savior. Ultimately her ability to experience peace and calm in her relationship with her husband would have less to do with changing her husband's terrible ways and more to do with changing her own focus. This revelation literally revolutionized her marriage!

Many times, in the middle of a difficult situation, discouragement and despair color a darker picture than reality. We get so focused on our problem that what seems minor to an objective observer looks gigantic to us. But as Quentin Crisp said, "The formula for achieving a successful relationship is simple: You should treat all disasters as if they were trivialities, but never treat a triviality as if it were a disaster."[2]

Oh, we of little faith! How easy it is to sink in fear of our circumstances and forget to see our Savior holding out his hand to us! If only we would remember that he is right there beside us, and he promises to never leave. As positive wives let's look to Jesus instead of focusing on our husbands' shortcomings. After all, only Jesus has the power to calm our marriage storms.

Win without a Word

Sharon's situation reminds me of an important truth about respect found in 1 Peter 3:1–2: "Wives, in the same way be submissive to your husbands so that, if any of them do not believe the word, they may be won over without words by the behavior of their wives, when they see the purity and reverence of your lives." I know we touched on the topic of submission in chapter 7, but I want us to focus on a different aspect of it here. In this verse Peter says that our purity and reverence as wives may just be the key factor that draws unbelieving husbands to the Lord. (If that's true, imagine what our purity and reverence could do in the hearts of believing husbands!)

We've said it before: A respectful attitude has a powerful impact. Imagine a married woman back in the early days of Christianity. She hears Paul preaching the gospel at the city gates, and her heart is touched. She decides to follow Christ. She returns home to her husband, a devout Jew, who is not convinced that Jesus is the Messiah. Would you think there'd be a little tension in that home? For sure!

What does Mrs. New Christian do? Her natural tendency might be to harp, nag, and do everything she can to show her husband how terribly wrong he is. But she takes a different track. She chooses to show respect to her husband out of obedience to God. She understands and respects the fact that he is not quite ready to receive Christ. She trusts his future to God's hands and lovingly carries out her daily role as a godly wife.

What happens in her husband's heart as he observes her beautiful behavior day after day? He begins to see the depth of real Christianity. He begins to feel the healing balm of the fruit of God's Spirit flowing through her: love, joy, peace, patience, kindness, goodness, faithfulness, gentleness, and self-control. These qualities begin to melt his heart and draw him to the Savior.

A mocking and scornful disposition is the opposite of respect and can be extremely destructive to a marriage. A wife's disrespectful attitude can actually send a husband further in the undesired direction, particularly when it comes to spiritual growth. A wife who nags or puts down her husband for not being "the spiritual leader" of the home often turns him further away from spiritual things. Why? Because it discourages him. It frustrates him and makes him feel as though he will never be good enough. When a wife respects her husband, however, she gently encourages him. When she makes an effort to point out something he is doing right rather than everything he is doing wrong, she has spurred him on to become a better man and a better husband.

What If He Never Changes?

Am I doomed to be stuck in this awful marriage for life? Believe it or not, this thought of despair enters the minds of many wives at one point or another in their marriages. When fearful, fretful, and despairing thoughts overtake us, we need to remember that they are from

Satan, the father of lies. As Christians we have the blessed assurance of knowing that God is the God of hope, redemption, and new life. He is able to resurrect a dead marriage. He is able to change sinful hearts and heal damaged lives. He is able to take a man headed down the road to destruction and turn him toward the path of light and life in Christ.

Will these things happen in your husband's life? I wish I could answer that! Only God sees the big picture from beginning to end; he knows things about your husband and your marriage that you and I don't. My faith tells me that God is able. But the fact of the matter is, he will never force himself on anyone.

This I *do* know: God is a God of hope. We must never place our hope in this world or in the people of this world; we must place our hope in ultimate victory beyond this world. Don't despair! God has not left you. His love, strength, and comfort are ever present. Your husband may change, or he may not change. Either way, the God of hope will never leave you. In the midst of your suffering and pain, he is close beside you. Feel his embrace. Allow his loving arms to give you warmth and comfort, healing and rest. Allow those same loving arms to hold you up when all seems lost.

There is hope in the God of hope! Romans 12:12 offers us positive strength and direction: "Be joyful in hope, patient in affliction, faithful in prayer." Be patient. Victory will come in God's timing, not yours. Remain joyful in hope and patient through your affliction—all the while holding up your husband and your marriage in prayer.

You may be thinking, *But you don't know how bad my husband is.* And you're right, I don't. But I do know there is *something* good about your husband. As a unique creation of God, he has something to offer this world. He can't be 100 percent evil personified! Instead of declaring how "bad" he is, why not begin looking for a glimmer of good? As someone once said, "When everything seems gray, look for the color."[3] Better yet, look for what God wants to teach you in your situation.

In her book *How to Act Right When Your Spouse Acts Wrong,* Leslie Vernick says that marriage often reveals things to us about ourselves that we may never have known otherwise. God uses relationships to sharpen us, as Proverbs 27:17 confirms. Leslie goes on to say:

> Instead of looking at what our spouse is doing that is upsetting, hurt-ful, or wrong to us, we must begin by redirecting our attention toward what our spouse's wrongs reveal in us. God may be using his or her imperfections, differences, weaknesses, and sins to teach us valuable lessons on how to forgive, how to forbear, how to have self-control, how to speak the truth in love, and how to love our enemies.[4]

Maybe—just maybe—God wants to use the challenges and diffi-culties we are facing with our husbands to chisel away some of our own weaknesses and flaws. Oh, the depth of growth we experience when we are cleansed through our trials! James's words to the early Christians apply so well to marriages: "Dear brothers and sisters, whenever trouble comes your way, let it be an opportunity for joy. For when your faith is tested, your endurance has a chance to grow. So let it grow, for when your endurance is fully developed, you will be strong in character and ready for anything" (James 1:2–4 NLT).

The refining that comes from being married to an imperfect person has lasting value. It's only in the process of shifting our focus from our husbands' faults to our Father's work that we truly become positive wives. We do less whining and more forgiving. Express less despair and more faith.

Maybe the challenge you face today is not about your husband and God as much as it is about you and God. What will you glean from this experience? My hope and my prayer is that you will emerge with a new vision, a new focus, a newly revived marriage, and a loving and lasting relationship with the One who loves you most dearly.

POWER POINT

⚙ **Read:** Genesis 12:10–20 and 1 Peter 3:6. Did Abram use good judgment in this situation? Who corrected the situation, God or Sarai (later called Sarah)? What does Peter have to say about Sarah's actions?

♡ **Pray:** Wonderful, redeeming heavenly Father, you are full of grace and mercy! Thank you for seeing past the muck, mire, and sin in my life to see my potential. Thank you for loving both my husband and me, and thank you for not being finished with the work you have begun in us. Help me to see past my husband's problems and recognize his potential. Keep my eyes focused on you and not on his failings. Help me to respect him unconditionally as my husband and your creation, and teach me how to honor him with my words and actions. Thank you for never leaving me and always caring for me. I love you, Lord. In Jesus' name I pray, amen.

💡 **Remember:** "Let us therefore make every effort to do what leads to peace and to mutual edification" (Romans 14:19).

☺ **Do:** Write your heart out. By this I mean write a prayer to God, asking him to help you work through the difficult issues of your marriage. Pour your heart out concerning your struggles to respect your husband, especially in the midst of his wrong behavior. Open your Bible to Psalm 40 and take in the healing words borne out of David's struggle.

Important note: If your husband's problems place you or your family in a serious or dangerous situation, please seek counseling and help immediately.

Power Principle #4

THe Power OF Encouragement

Encourage one another and build each other up,
just as in fact you are doing.

—1 Thessalonians 5:11

Encouragement is oxygen to the soul.

—George Matthew Adams

Word Power Made Easy
Doling Out Delicious Morsels of Good Words

There are high spots in all of our lives, and most of them have come
about through encouragement from someone else.

—George Matthew Adams

Here's a little riddle: What weapon is powerful enough to
pierce the heart with a single blow, yet sweet enough to soothe a
hurting soul? If you guessed the weapon of your words, you're right.
Solomon tells us, "Pleasant words are a honeycomb, sweet to the soul
and healing to the bones" (Proverbs 16:24). He also says, "Reckless words
pierce like a sword" (Proverbs 12:18).

Rarely do people stop long enough to consider the power of their
words. But as positive wives, we must. We need to recognize that what
we say can have a significant, lasting impact on others—especially
our spouses. If we choose to speak encouraging words, we can build
better marriage relationships, lift up our husbands, and help them to
reach greater heights. As Scudder N. Parker has said, "People have a
way of becoming what you encourage them to be—not what you nag
them to be."[1]

Deep in our hearts we know we need to be encouraging wives; but
somewhere between laundry, errands, work, housework, and meal
preparation, we lose the energy and motivation to build up our
spouses. Even when our lives are not so busy, we tend to forget the

importance of affirmation in marriage. Well, this chapter is a reminder! And as we go along, we'll talk about practical ways we can encourage our husbands with our words.

Daily Vitamins

Do you take your daily dose of vitamins to help you stay healthy? I hope so. The immediate and long-term effects of proper nutrition can't be underestimated. I remember when I first started taking vitamins, I had to consciously remind myself to take them. Now it's second nature. In fact, since I usually go into the kitchen and down them almost without thinking, I find myself having to try to remember if I took them in order to keep from taking them twice.

Words of encouragement are a lot like vitamins. Our husbands need them to stay healthy. When we first begin giving out daily doses of encouragement, we may need to remind ourselves to dole them out each day. But once encouragement becomes a habit, positive, life-giving words will flow out of our hearts and off our tongues more naturally.

In his portrait of a noble wife in Proverbs 31, Solomon says, "She opens her mouth with skillful and godly Wisdom, and in her tongue is the law of kindness" (Proverbs 31:26 AMP). Could others say that about us—that we open our mouths with "skillful and godly wisdom"? When I think of the word *skillful,* I think of construction rather than destruction. This noble woman uses her words to build up the people around her, not tear them down.

And what about the second part of that verse? Could people say that the "law of kindness" is on our tongues? In other words, does kindness rule what we say to the point that kind words flow naturally? The noble woman of Proverbs 31 gave up discouraging words long ago; her tongue is ruled by kindness, thoughtfulness, and courtesy. Kind, encouraging words are what the people around her have come to expect.

What rules our tongues on a daily basis? Blessings or curses? Compliments or complaints? Praise or discouragement? The fact is, our words are an overflow of our hearts. As positive wives, we need to intentionally turn our hearts and minds toward God's goodness and kindness every day. How? A daily devotional time is a great way to keep our hearts pointed toward Christ. Only God can heal our hearts and make them fresh and new and full of gratitude. By spending quality time with him each day, we can begin to speak words that flow from healthy hearts and tongues guided by his love.

If you're like me, you want to speak encouraging words to your husband—words that flow from a healthy, renewed heart—but sometimes you need a reminder. There are days I can't remember what I walked to the other end of the house for; how am I going to remember to encourage my spouse? I've found that writing myself a note helps. I place the note in my makeup drawer; it's a perfect spot since I open the drawer almost every morning. Besides, I like knowing that I'm the only one who will see the note there. (What's the best place for your note? Perhaps in your Bible or journal, so you'll see it when you have your morning devotional time.)

For me, bright and happy work best; so I've taken a round, yellow sticky note, put a big smiley face in the center, and have written these words: "Curt's Daily Booster." One glance into my makeup drawer is all I need to remind myself to give Curt a delicious morsel of encouragement sometime throughout the day—maybe a "thank you" for his willingness to get up early to go to work and provide for the family. An expression of kindness and support when he comes home frustrated or discouraged. An "I'm proud of you" when he reaches a goal or does something well.

Buzzards and Bees

Often we get so tuned in to what our husbands do wrong that we don't even think to encourage them for the good things they do. But if we will start noticing and encouraging our husbands' positive qualities, many of the negatives will begin to diminish and take care of themselves. Johann von Goethe put it well when he said, "Correction does much, but encouragement does more."[2]

Shirley Boone gives this advice to positive wives: "Be to his virtues very kind. Be to his faults a little blind." She says the difference between focusing on the positive and negative traits in our husbands is like the difference between the feeding patterns of buzzards and bees. Think about it. Buzzards fly high up in the sky, searching for dead prey. When they find a dead and decaying carcass, they swoop down to devour it. Honeybees, in contrast, only look for sweet nectar. They search through gardens filled with flowers, using very discriminating taste.

Buzzards produce only one thing: fear. Honeybees, on the other hand, produce honeycombs that drip with sweetness and give pleasure and sustenance to many. Both bees and buzzards find what they are seeking. So do spouses. If we are focused on our husbands' faults, we'll find them every time. But if we're set on finding our husbands' strengths—if we're actively seeking out their goodness—we will find that too. How sweet a relationship can become when both spouses are looking for the nectar of one another's positive qualities!

Buzzards and bees cannot choose their instincts; they simply do what they do. But the good news for us is, we are not bound by instinct. We can choose each and every day to focus on the good in our husbands and ignore the negatives.[3]

Many of us struggle with this choice because, frankly, it's easier to be critical. In her book *A Closer Walk*, best-selling author Catherine Marshall reveals a particular time in her life when God taught her a lesson about criticism. We would do well to learn from her experience! Here is an excerpt from her book:

> One morning last week He (the Lord) gave me an assignment: for one day I was to go on a "fast" from criticism. I was not to criticize anybody about anything.
>
> Into my mind crowded all the usual objections. "But then what happens to value judgments? You Yourself, Lord, spoke of 'righteous judgment.' How could society operate without standards and limits?"
>
> All such resistance was brushed aside. "Just obey Me without questioning: an absolute fast on any critical statement for this day."
>
> As I pondered this assignment, I realized there was an even humorous side to this kind of fast. What did the Lord want to show me?
>
> For the first half of the day, I simply felt a void, almost as if I had been wiped out as a person. This was especially true at lunch with my husband, Len, my mother, son Jeff, and my secretary Jeanne Sevigny, present. Several topics came up...about which I had definite opinions. I listened to the others and kept silent. Barbed comments on the tip of my tongue about certain world leaders were suppressed. In our talkative family no one seemed to notice.
>
> Bemused, I noticed that my comments were not missed. The federal government, the judicial system, and the institutional church could apparently get along fine without my penetrating observations. But still I didn't see what this fast on criticism was accomplishing—until mid-afternoon.
>
> For several years I had been praying for one talented young man whose life had gotten sidetracked. Perhaps my prayers for him had been too negative. That afternoon, a specific, positive vision

I can live for two months on a good compliment. —Mark Twain

ッ

for this life was dropped into my mind with God's unmistakable hallmark on it—joy.

Ideas began to flow in a way I had not experienced in years. Now it was apparent what the Lord wanted me to see. My critical nature had not corrected a single one of the multitudinous things I found fault with. What it had done was to stifle my own creativity— in prayer, in relationships, perhaps even in writing-ideas that He wanted to give me.

What He is showing me so far can be summed up as follows:

1. A critical spirit focuses us on ourselves and makes us unhappy. We lose perspective and humor.

2. A critical spirit blocks the positive, creative thoughts God longs to give us.

3. A critical spirit can prevent good relationships between individuals and often produces retaliatory criticalness.

4. Criticalness blocks the work of the Spirit of God: love, good will, and mercy.

5. Whenever we see something genuinely wrong in another person's behavior, rather than criticize him or her directly, or—far worse—gripe about him behind his back, we should ask the Spirit of God to do the correction needed.[4]

When we choose, like Catherine Marshall, to fast from criticism, does that mean we must not admonish a person who is clearly in the wrong? Certainly not! When an issue arises, the right thing to do is to discuss it directly, respectfully, and humbly. The lesson Catherine learned (and one we all could benefit from) is that a *critical spirit* has little use. When we are preoccupied with our husbands' faults, it is very difficult to see their potential and offer positive encouragement. But if we refuse to give in to a critical spirit and determine instead to build on our spouses' strengths, we're sure to see some of their weaknesses fade away in the process.

What It Is and What It's Not

How would you define encouragement? Some people think of encouragement as kind but empty words designed to make others feel better about themselves. Nothing could be further from the truth! Actually, the word *encourage* means to give courage and strength to another person. It is sincere and honest help. When Joshua was taking over the leadership of the Israelites (not a job to relish), God offered these words of encouragement:

> Be strong and courageous, because you will lead these people to inherit the land I swore to their forefathers to give them. Be strong and very courageous. Be careful to obey all the law my servant Moses gave you; do not turn from it to the right or to the left, that you may be successful wherever you go. Do not let this Book of the Law depart from your mouth; meditate on it day and night, so that you may be careful to do everything written in it. Then you will be prosperous and successful. Have I not commanded you? Be strong and courageous. Do not be terrified; do not be discouraged, for the LORD your God will be with you wherever you go. (Joshua 1:6–9)

Wow! God is the ultimate encourager, isn't he? He not only offered strength and courage to Joshua, he offered direction too. His words were far from empty; on the contrary, they were filled with truth and light. As we walk in God's ways and allow his Spirit to flow through us, you and I can follow our heavenly Father's example and use our words to give courage, strength, truth, and light.

Encouraging words are not flattery. Far from it. Flattery can be described as excessive, insincere praise or an exaggerated compliment. Like the simulated buildings on the set of a movie, flattery is a fake facade. Proverbs 29:5 says, "Whoever flatters his neighbor is spreading a net for his feet." In other words, when we use flattery, we usually have a hidden agenda. We're trying to get someone to do something for us. We're not sincerely giving encouragement; we're serving ourselves—and more often than not, our strategy backfires. Words of encouragement must be built on the foundation of truth, or they won't be received or believed.

It helps to be specific. "Have a great day," is a nice, encouraging phrase. But "I hope your appointment goes well today—the Wilsons are fortunate to have a financial planner like you!" is likely to have a greater impact. In order to be specific, we must be observant. What do our husbands need at this moment? What words of encouragement will give them the strength to go forward?

God knows best. When you don't know what to say, ask God to give you the right words. He knows exactly how you can encourage and strengthen your spouse. Pray, "Lord, give me the right words to encourage my husband today." As we pray for our husbands on a daily basis, God often opens our eyes and shows us our husbands' needs. Then we can open our mouths with confidence, speaking the right words that will encourage and strengthen them for whatever lies ahead.

Variety Is the Spice of Life

The spoken word is only one way to offer encouragement to our husbands. We can also use the written word. For example, I like to send Curt e-mails now and then. Sometimes I put sticky-note messages on his mirror or in his briefcase before he goes to work. I'm always looking for new and creative ways to give him a little blessing and boost in his otherwise ordinary day.

Pleasant words are a honeycomb, sweet to the soul and healing to the bones. —Proverbs 16:24

Twice a year I spend way too much on greeting cards. The local Hallmark store makes a killing off me around Valentine's Day and my wedding anniversary in late July, because I take great joy and pleasure in searching for cards to send to Curt. About two weeks before Valentine's Day, I begin sending fun and romantic cards to him at his office (marked "personal"). I do the same leading up to our anniversary. It's my way of encouraging him and letting him know that he is my hero and my main attraction.

In addition to being creative in our methods, we should also use variety in the things we say. Our husbands need encouragement in many different areas of their lives. They need affirmation about their physical looks, their work, what they do at home, their friendships, the way they handle the family finances, and more. Why should we get stuck giving the same encouragement over and over when we have so many areas to choose from each day? If we will use a little variety, our daily dose of encouragement can always be fresh, new, and real.

Sometimes the best way to encourage our husbands in a particular area is to let them know we see their potential. They may be focused on where they are at this moment; our job is to focus on where they can go from here. We can offer strengthening words, such as, "You are gifted with incredible creativity. Keep at it, and I know your diligent work will eventually pay off." Or, "You have great leadership skills. I know the company will recognize it, so hang in there."

Try beginning your encouragement with a "you" statement, such as:

- You are strong...
- You are smart...
- You are creative...
- You are handsome...
- You are well liked...

Then complete the thought with a positive, strength-giving comment:

- I believe you can ...
- I'm sure it will...
- I know you're able...
- My hope is that ...
- I can see you doing...

You may be surprised at the power of one statement of real encouragement. We are told in Hebrews 3:13 to "encourage one another daily." As positive wives we must be about God's business of building up the body of believers—and we must begin with our own husbands.

The Power of a Wife's Words

The following thoughts have been quoted often concerning life in general, but I think they apply particularly to marriage:

- The five most important words are: "I have confidence in you."
- The four most important words: "What is your opinion?"
- The three most important words: "If you please."
- The two most important words: "Thank you."
- The most important word: "We."
- The least important word: "I."[5]

In marriage we come together to build each other up. You may be thinking, *But my husband doesn't build me up. No fair!* Let me encourage you: Begin the process anyway. The spirit of encouragement is contagious! Yes, we ought to give encouragement as a gift, expecting nothing in return; but we shouldn't be surprised when positive results come back to us. Let's be faithful to pass on the blessed gift of encouragement to our husbands. As we have freely received, so may we freely give.

POWER POINT

⚙ **Read:** James 3:3–12. What are the analogies James uses to demonstrate the power of the tongue? What does James say we can we do with our words, both positively and negatively? Read verse 8 again and couple it with Matthew 19:26. Describe the only way a tongue can be tamed.

♡ **Pray:** Wonderful heavenly Father, you are the Great Encourager, and I praise you for your loving-kindness toward us. Thank you for being the giver of strength and courage. I am so grateful for the way you are at work in my life and the life of my husband! Thank you for his good qualities, and yes, thank you for his weaknesses too. Keep me from having a critical spirit, and help me to focus on my husband's strengths. Give me words to speak that will encourage his heart. Help me to be a blessing to him, building him up and helping him to be the best he can be. In Jesus' name I pray, amen.

💡 **Remember:** "Do not let any unwholesome talk come out of your mouths, but only what is helpful for building others up according to their needs, that it may benefit those who listen" (Ephesians 4:29).

☺ **Do:** Place a note somewhere in your house where you (and only you) will see it on a daily basis, reminding yourself to speak at least one word of encouragement to your husband each day. Make a deliberate effort to build your marriage by encouraging your husband in sincere and creative ways. Visit a greeting-card store this week and find a card to give him. Write an uplifting message inside that builds up his good qualities.

Extraordinary Companionship
Enjoying Life, Love, and Laughter Together

*Love is the expansion of two natures in such a fashion that
each includes the other, each is enriched by the other.*

—Felix Adler

Henrietta and her husband, Wally, had struggled for years
with a troubled marriage. The owner of the only bank in town,
Wally was also the town's most tight-fisted miser. His constant insis-
tence that Henrietta curb her spending, along with his relentless bargain hunting, nearly drove his wife crazy.

Much to her surprise one day, Henrietta found a note addressed to
her on her doorstep. "Leave ten thousand dollars under the roots of the
dogwood tree in the town square tonight," the note said, "or your husband will be kidnapped, and you will never see him again." That night
Henrietta went to the town square and left her reply under the dogwood tree: "I don't have even a hundred dollars, let alone ten thousand,
but I am counting on you boys to keep your end of the deal."

Okay, so no marriage is perfect! Henrietta's solution to her troubled
marriage was creative, I have to admit; but hopefully you and I have
better, more positive options available to us. No matter what condition
our marriages are in, we have one common ground we can build on:
the basic human need for companionship. Going back to the Garden
of Eden, we see that men and women were created to be relational

153

beings. It was not good for man to be alone, so woman was created to be his companion. Pete Briscoe, pastor of Bent Tree Bible Fellowship in Dallas, says that the word *helper* used in Genesis 2:20 actually means "rescuer." What did the woman rescue the man from? Briscoe answers in one word: "Loneliness."[1]

The word *companion* comes from the Latin root words *com,* meaning "with," and *panis,* meaning "bread." The picture we get is of a messmate, someone with whom we break bread. Our souls long for such a companion—for someone with whom we can have the kind of intimate fellowship that shares not only meals but lives. Ultimately this longing is what draws husbands and wives together in marriage. As wives we can choose to build upon this common need and deepen our relationships, or we can choose to ignore this need and create a growing chasm between us and our spouses. I don't know about you, but I vote for option number one. Our marriages can grow so much richer and deeper if we'll choose to experience companionship in a loving and vibrant way.

Creative Fun

Men and women have certain innate differences in the way they build and develop relationships. Generally speaking, women tend to deepen relationships by talking together with their companions. Men, on the other hand, bond by doing things together. According to author Leil Lowndes, "A man wants a woman who enjoys the same activities, one he can have fun with. He likes to feel they can play tennis, go to concerts or basketball games or movies, or just sit at home and be side-by-side couch potatoes. Doing things together is important to a woman too, but it's higher on the male wish list."[2]

One of the main ways we can deepen our relationships with our spouses is to discover creative ways to enjoy each other's company.

Companionship develops as we find activities that we have fun doing together. Of course, that's not always easy. As men and women are innately different, we may not necessarily enjoy doing all of the same things. Some activities are definitely best left to time with our girl-friends (shopping for shoes, going to "girl movies," enjoying afternoon tea at the Ritz). But there are many activities we can enjoy with our husbands if we're willing to meet them halfway.

I'm not gifted in the area of home decorating, but Curt loves it. (I know; it's usually the other way around.) In fact, Curt loves to shop for antique furniture. When we were first married, we visited antique shops, sales, and auctions together, thriftily buying furniture for our first home. I had to stretch myself quite a bit, but I was happy to be spending time with Curt. Over the years I have found my niche at the antique stores: I love to look for old books and English teacups. Whenever we travel (or even on some Saturdays at home in Dallas) we like to hit the antique stores together, Curt looking for furniture and me for books and teacups. I suppose you could say we have found our cup of tea!

Sports can be a great way to develop companionship. Some sports may be enjoyed best between husbands and their buddies, but other sports can be enjoyed as a couple. For example, our friends Sherry and Dale never miss a Dallas Cowboys football home game. They love it. It's their spectator sport to enjoy together. Dale faithfully plays golf with "the guys" every week, and Sherry loves getting together with her girlfriends for Bible study; but a Cowboys game is a Sherry-and-Dale thing.

A few nights ago, as we were driving home from a family sports activity, Curt must have repeated the phrase "That was so much fun" at least four times! I had to smile, because he was right. Understand, I was not initially excited about participating in this sport. It's not typically a women's sport. But now that I've been doing it for some time, I'm hooked. I love it, and Curt loves that I love it! I'm just glad that one evening several months ago I was open to Curt's suggestion that I go with him and try it.

"What sport?" you may be asking. Well, if you must know: it's skeet and trap shooting. You heard me. Shooting little round sporting clays with a shotgun. You're not going to believe this, but I even asked Curt for a shotgun for Christmas. (Of course he was thrilled at the request.) To think that we have been married for twenty years, and we have just discovered a new activity we can do together!

All this to say, don't close the door on new activities. You may be surprised. Try it, you may like it; and if you don't, move on. The important thing is to be continually open to ways you can share companionship with your husband. Many women take up golf after retirement in order to spend time with their husbands and to have something in common they can do at home or on vacations. Here's a hint: Make sure your husband *wants* you to take up the sport with him. He may need his "buddy time." Communication is the key. Explore, discuss, try out, and enjoy new activities together throughout your marriage. You're never too old to learn something new or take up a fresh interest.

Creative Work

In Proverbs 18:24 Solomon says that a man of many companions comes to ruin. Why? Because it is difficult for us to invest our time, energy, and commitment into numerous lives. When it comes to relationships, depth is to be valued over volume. In terms of priority, we must devote ourselves first to the Lord, then to our relationships with our husbands, then to other relationships.

Companionship is fun, but it is also work. Building any relationship takes energy and effort—and all the more so if the relationship is for the long haul. We must continually choose creativity over complacency if we want to build a deep and satisfying companionship that lasts a lifetime. I hear many women say, "But I'm just not the creative type." That's okay. There are plenty of books, videos, and other resources out there to give you ideas.

Of course the primary resource we have is God, the Creator of the universe. That means the work of companionship must involve prayer. Our number one job as creative companions is to prayerfully seek God's imaginative wisdom for building our marriages. God knows our husbands better than we know them—even better than they know themselves. If we ask, he will help us identify fresh and new ways to deepen our harmony and companionship with our spouses.

Dates with a Purpose

One way we can strengthen our companionship with our spouses is by planning dates. Dating is not just for couples who are courting. Fun, romantic, purposeful dates are important for married couples too.

Be deliberate about scheduling a date with your spouse at least once a month. Put it on the calendar or it won't happen. A date doesn't have to be scheduled for the evening; many times Curt and I meet for lunch on a weekday while the kids are in school. Sometimes on Saturday mornings we walk to a nearby health club, work out together, and then go out for breakfast.

What about the kids? Baby-sitters can come from many different sources. Certainly having family nearby is helpful when it comes to finding a sitter you know and trust. But if family is not an option, consider trading with another couple—one Friday night you watch their kids, and the next Friday night they watch yours. My sister does this with a family at her church. The kids love it as much as the parents because they get to be with their friends.

Best friends make the best spouses. —Wilfred A. Peterson

ᶜ:

Years ago when I was in need of a baby-sitter, I put a note on the bulletin board at a nearby Christian school. Try it—it works! Not only will you find wonderful teenagers who are ready and willing to earn some extra money, you may discover some young teachers who would be blessed by the opportunity. Put the word out at your church youth group too. You'll discover many wonderful people who are available to help you out and be positive role models for your kids in the process.

Communication is the key to a great date. Talk over the plans with your husband and agree to do something that you would both find enjoyable. As in other areas of your relationship, a little give-and-take from both parties may be necessary. But don't try to push an idea that your husband sincerely hates. Be understanding of his feelings and realize that you have to let go of some ideas (like taking him to the opera). He may never want to do certain things that you want to do. But then again, he probably has some ideas that you don't want to do either (like going to a wrestling match). Compromise where you can and release the rest.

Here's a list of ideas to help you plan creative and memorable dates:

Saturday-morning breakfast. Plan to enjoy Saturday-morning breakfast together at least once a month at your favorite breakfast restaurant. (You may want to choose a location within walking distance and enjoy the benefits of a good walk too). If you can't get away from the house due to baby-sitting challenges, enjoy your favorite breakfast together out on the back porch without the kids. Tell them this is Mommy and Daddy's own private breakfast. Use this time to talk about the previous week and your plans for the upcoming week. Encourage each other, listen to each other, pray for each other.

Retro date. Think back to one of your favorite dinner dates from those blissful days of courting. If you can, go back to the exact same restaurant; if not, go to one that is similar. Over dinner, talk about what it was that attracted you to each other in the first place. After dinner rent one of the movies you saw and enjoyed when you were dating, or purchase a CD with music from your dating years and listen to it while you drive.

Favorites night. Let him choose his favorite restaurant and/or movie for your date. On your next date, you choose. Whoever makes the choice creates the plan for the whole evening, buys the tickets, makes the reservation, and so on. Build the intrigue and anticipation by keeping your plan a secret until you go. Try to outdo each other.

Coffee house and browse. Many bookstores now include a coffee bar, so a special and inexpensive date can include both browsing and sipping. Look at some travel books to plan your next vacation, check out the latest bestsellers, look for a book on a shared interest you have, or help each other find books on one another's interests.

Sunday-afternoon relaxation. Sunday is a wonderful day of relaxation, rest, and renewal. Now and then the afternoon should be reserved for some special husband-and-wife time. Be sensitive to your spouse's interests, since this can be a much-needed day of respite from his normal routine. If he enjoys looking at homes, go to a few Open Houses. Go to a park and read, or watch a sports event together. Talk about the week ahead and pray together about the coming activities.

Museum date. Are there any good museums in your hometown or in a city nearby? Often we neglect to visit the museums close to us. Strolling through a museum, whether small or large, can make an interesting and inexpensive date. Find some brochures or do a little research about the museums in your area, then discuss with your husband which ones you may have an interest in visiting together. Be willing to stretch and step out of your comfort zone. Perhaps you can choose the Baseball Hall of Fame for him one month and the Arboretum for you the next month.

Picnic in the park. Choose a beautiful time of year to go on a picnic together. In Texas the summers are unbearably hot, but late fall and early spring are lovely times to go to the park. Pack a basket with your favorite beverage and snacks. Bring along a Frisbee or some books to enjoy in the fresh air of the great outdoors.

Cook by the book. Pull out your favorite cookbook and decide together on a recipe to cook. Run to the grocery store, get the ingredients, and then chop, sauté, and grate together to create a magnificent meal. If your husband's not the cooking type, this may take some initial convincing. But he'll be surprised at how much fun cooking together can be.

Sports event. Go to a sporting event, or watch one on television together. It doesn't have to be your favorite sport in order for you to enjoy it. You may want to choose one of your favorite sporting events on one date and one of his favorites on another date. The event doesn't need to be major league. Try a high-school football game, a local hockey team game, or a club tennis match.

If you and your husband enjoy playing a particular sport together—say, tennis or golf or skeet shooting—set a play date. But remember, while husbands love companionship, there are certain sports your husband may prefer to play only with the guys. Don't force yourself into that picture. (I'll never forget the *I Love Lucy* show in which Lucy and Ethel decided to learn to play golf with the boys, and Ricky and Fred tried to sabotage the lessons by teaching them some ridiculously wrong rules.)

Walking date. Walking is not only good for your health; it's good for your relationship with your spouse. As you walk and talk together, you have each other's undivided attention. You can cover subjects that the hustle of the daily routine often keeps you from discussing. The best part is that you are being active (oxygen is flowing to the brain for clearer thinking), and you're getting exercise together (which can be much more appealing to a man than just sitting and talking). If your schedules and kids allow, you can have this date nearly every night!

Gift night. Decide on a certain amount of money you can afford to spend on the date, split it in two, then go to the mall. With your half, you buy something for your husband that you know he would like. With his half, he buys *you* a special gift. As you shop together, you both have the right to veto a gift before it's purchased, and you can give hints about your preferences. The one rule is that you cannot say outright, "I want this." Laugh, giggle, hint, flirt, and enjoy giving and receiving your gifts.

Dessert date. Sometimes it's fun to go out for a piece of pie or a chocolate sundae together. Yes, splurge! Keep the conversation light and full of laughter. Enjoy your sweetie as much as you enjoy the sweets. If you can't find a baby-sitter, wait until the kids go to bed and have a "Make Your Own Sundae" party.

Dreamy Vacations

Taking family vacations is important, but taking trips that are for just the two of you is important too. Consider taking an anniversary trip each year—even if it's just for a night or two in a hotel in the next town. Being together for more than twenty-four hours tends to bring good things to the surface. Difficult issues may surface too; but a trip together is a healthy time to face each other, experience each other, and grow together without the influence of kids or other people. Make use of nearby grandparents or trade off with another couple to work out the baby-sitting needs. We have some wonderful young couples in our church that we pay to help us out sometimes.

Vacations don't have to be expensive. Look for cheap airfares, hotel deals, and rental car offers. Book on-line using resources such as hotels.com, priceline.com, and travelocity.com. Sometimes I've found an airline's best offers by going directly to its own Web page.

Here's a list of some potential vacation ideas:

Hometown hotel. Sometimes it can be fun to go on a vacation right in your own hometown. Simply getting away from the responsibilities of home and kids can bring renewal and refreshment to your routines and your relationship. Order room service. Put on the hotel robes and snuggle up to watch a pay-per-view movie. Enjoy the pool or Jacuzzi. Relax!

Bed-and-breakfast getaway. Often inexpensive and quaint, a bed-and-breakfast can be a delightful change of pace. Check out some of the bed-and-breakfasts in nearby small towns and choose one for a quick weekend getaway. You'll find that the innkeepers are very helpful in directing you to local shops, museums, activities, and sights. One of our favorite places is a bed-and-breakfast in Granbury, Texas, just about two hours from our house. The town of Granbury has a picturesque town square filled with antique shops (you know us!) and quaint restaurants. My favorite thing about Granbury is that it's one of the few towns in America that still has a drive-in movie theater. Romantic fun!

Capitol idea. Have you ever considered visiting the capitol buildings in each state you travel through? Choose a new state capitol to visit each year, starting with your own state. Ask a passerby to take a picture of you and your husband standing on the steps of the capitol building. Take a tour and learn some history about that city and state. You may even want to write ahead of time and arrange to have a state representative show you around. Find out the state motto and write it in your memory book next to your picture. You'll find that most state mottos have a powerful message for us all.

Favorites vacation. Take turns choosing your ideal vacation (sticking, of course, within your set budget). One year it's his turn to secretly plan the vacation, make the reservations, and do the research on hotels, restaurants, activities, and events. The next year you're the trip coordinator. Whether you choose to get away for a week or a weekend, you add variety, intrigue, and excitement when you take turns planning. Early in our marriage, Curt and I took turns planning short trips. I would plan a short, but sweet, Valentine weekend getaway, and Curt would plan one for our anniversary. By taking turns, each of us had a sense of ownership and a sense of service. We had a chance to get our own ways, but we also found ourselves considering not just what we wanted, but what would bless the other one.

Best beach. Are you beach people? Plan a trip each year to a different beach in the United States, with the goal of discovering the best beach in the nation. Create your own ranking system. After several years of beach exploration, return to your favorite beach. Whatever beach you visit, take long walks along the water's edge. Beach walking is great exercise (so you don't have to worry about what you eat at dinner); it's also a wonderful and romantic opportunity to talk and just be together. If you're not beach bums, consider finding the best ski slope, the best hot tub, or the best Marriott in the nation. The fun never stops!

Three-city tour. Choose an area of the nation where you can plan a three-city adventure. For instance, along the southern coast of California, you could start in San Diego, move on up to Laguna Beach, and spend your final stretch in Santa Barbara. On the other side of the country, you could start at Amelia Island in Florida, move up to Sea Island in Georgia, and finish the trip in Savannah or Charleston.

Route 66. Check out the vacation opportunities along the historic and famous Route 66. Visit towns like Santa Monica. See the Grand Canyon. Long car trips are great for seeing the sights and just being together. Bring along some of your favorite CDs or tapes for the trip. Consider some of the coastal highways or mountain arteries (such as the Blue Ridge Parkway) for other car adventures.

Follow your team. Are you big fans of a certain athletic team? Travel to an away game together. Or travel to another city to see a performance by your favorite entertainer.

Home hideaway. Sometimes money is tight, and a trip is just not possible. Take the time off anyway and enjoy a vacation hideaway in your own home. Send your kids to their grandparents' house or to the home of good friends for a few days. Resist the temptation to take care of household responsibilities and try not to answer the phone. Discover the fun things you and your husband can do in your own city, using one or more of the date suggestions mentioned above.

Other Encouragers

Extraordinary companionship doesn't only develop from the dates you go on and the vacations you take; it is also encouraged by the little things you do for one another day by day. Here are some things to incorporate into your relationship on a regular basis:

Look at each other. Studies show that lingering eye contact creates a bond between two people. Never underestimate the power of the eyes! As Solomon wrote, "Bright eyes gladden the heart" (Proverbs 15:30 NASB). Elsewhere he said, "Let your eyes look straight ahead, fix your gaze directly before you" (Proverbs 4:25). And in Song of Songs, he wrote, "You have stolen my heart, my sister, my bride; you have stolen my heart with one glance of your eyes" (Song of Songs 4:9).

Solomon also gave a sincere warning to men concerning an adulterous woman, saying, "Do not lust in your heart after her beauty or let her captivate you with her eyes" (Proverbs 6:25). If anyone is going to captivate your husband with her eyes, it had better be you! Look lovingly into your husband's eyes, letting him know that he is adored and esteemed. Allow your gaze to linger. Study his face.

Obviously you can't gaze at one another when you're walking or driving. There is a time and a place for everything. An eye embrace can come over dinner or coffee. If you're in the car, it can come after you've parked. Look for the opportunities that invite themselves, but be subtle, not obvious; be interesting, not overbearing.

Touch each other. Touching offers another opportunity to bond in a nonverbal way. A simple touch is an encouragement to your spouse, letting him know you notice him and are interested in him. I'm not talking about touching in a sexual way as much as in a flirting way. A simple pat, a brush of your hand on his arm or thigh, or a hug now and then can put a spark back in your love relationship. Give him a spontaneous backrub or hold his hand on a walk. Become aware of the ways your husband likes to be touched and the ways he doesn't.

Smile at each other. When is the last time you smiled at your husband? I realize there are times when we don't feel like smiling, but I think we miss many opportunities to offer our spouses the gift of a smile. Remember the story I told in chapter 8 about my determination to greet Curt with a smile when he comes in the door after work? That's one great time to offer a smile, but there are no doubt many other times—say, when you're in a conversation or enjoying a sport together—that you can throw a smile in your husband's direction. A smile lets him know you are enjoying your time together and not just surviving it. It gives him encouragement and strength, along with the sense that you support him and want to be with him.

"A smile speaks a thousand words," I often tell women's groups. It's like nonverbal sunshine! Solomon knew this when he wrote, "A cheerful heart is good medicine" (Proverbs 17:22). Throw a smile in your husband's direction a few times each day, and watch what it does for your marriage!

Look for times to simply be together. Curt and I enjoy spending time together sitting side by side and reading the newspaper on the back porch. We don't talk; we simply enjoy one another's company in the solitude and beauty of the backyard as we sip coffee and read. There is something significant and special about our shared time together, even though we're not interacting. What opportunities do you have for this kind of nonverbal time with your husband? I've heard many husbands say they would love for their wives to simply sit down and watch television with them every once in a while. If your husband likes to watch TV to relax, by all means stop your busy-ness now and then, sit down next to him on the couch, and enjoy a program together.

Connect spiritually. Sharing on a spiritual level will bond you and your husband in a deep way. Pray together for your family, for your future plans and upcoming activities, and for your relationship. Thank God for his blessings and for the good qualities you see in one another. Enjoy spiritual fellowship together. Even if your husband is not a Christian, he may still be willing to pray with you now and then or read a verse or proverb from the Bible together. It wouldn't hurt to ask!

Perhaps you're thinking, *My husband is a Christian, but he's definitely not the spiritual leader of our home. There's no way we can bond spiritually.* Many women feel this way. What can you do? First and foremost, remember that you're not your husband's Holy Spirit. If you try to be, you're likely to get the exact opposite of the result you're looking for. Instead, gently encourage your spouse. Ask him if you could pray a short prayer together before you go to bed at night. If he says no, don't get upset. Give him time and allow God to draw him to the point of desiring prayer.

Several years ago I was feeling spiritually dry, so I asked Curt if he would help me by reading aloud from the Bible as we sat on the back porch. He not only read it; he began to talk about the truths in the verses. I believe that spontaneous, spiritual time together was just as much a blessing for him as it was for me. You can't demand that your husband join with you spiritually, but you can humbly make suggestions as opportunities arise. Keep looking for those opportunities!

How can you experience extraordinary companionship with your spouse? Find fun things to do together. Keep going on dates. Plan vacations. Spend time together gazing into one another's eyes, holding hands, and simply enjoying quiet moments. Pray together. By investing in your relationship this way, every year of your marriage will be sweeter than the one before.

POWER POINT

⚙ **Read:** Acts 18:1–4, 18; Romans 16:3–4; 1 Corinthians 16:19; 2 Timothy 4:19. Make a list of the variety of activities Aquila and Priscilla engaged in together. What effect do you think these shared efforts had on their marriage? How did God use their companionship for his glory?

♡ **Pray:** Holy Father, I praise you for your magnificent creative power. Thank you for loving me and living within me. You are my constant companion and friend! Please help me to enjoy my relationship with my husband and show me new and creative ways to develop our companionship more fully. Deepen the love and delight we have in each other. Enrich our marriage with a deep, bonding friendship that lasts a lifetime. Thank you for working so mightily in our hearts and lives. In Jesus' name I pray, amen.

💡 **Remember:** "Behold, how good and how pleasant it is for brethren to dwell together in unity!" (Psalm 133:1 AMP).

☺ **Do:** Grab your calendar and a pen right now. Go ahead; I'll wait. Now plot several potential date nights on the calendar for this month. Talk to your husband and have him choose the one that works best for him. Look over the creative date ideas provided in this chapter and choose one that you and your husband would enjoy (or create one of your own). On your date, remember to gaze, touch, smile, and discuss plans for a vacation for just the two of you.

THe Power oF Physical Attraction

How beautiful you are and how pleasing, O love, with your delights!

—Song of Songs 7:6

We are born with a deep longing for and appreciation of beauty. Our spirits are drawn to it. It calls to us, nourishes us, stimulates us.

—Nancy Stafford

Beauty Inside Out
Discovering the Beautiful You

A thing of beauty is a joy forever.

—John Keats

Early each December I begin the annual wrapping experience. Of course, I'm still wrapping the last presents at 11:55 P.M. on December 24 like everyone else; but I do try to get a head start on a few presents. Does it ever bother you that by 10:30 A.M. on December 25, all the beautiful wrapping work you've done is torn up, strewn across the floor, or stuffed in trash bags? I find it a little frustrating that I pour time, money, and talent into Christmas gift wrapping, yet I have never had a child (or adult, for that matter) hold the wrapped present in his or her hands and exclaim, "Wow, what a lovely package! I'm not even going to open it. I think I will just enjoy the wrapping. Who cares about the present?"

No, that scenario has never happened in our house. What about yours? The truth is that no matter how beautiful the wrapping is, the present is what counts. So why put so much effort into the wrapping? I can think of a few reasons. A nicely wrapped gift builds anticipation and intrigue for what's inside. It says to the receiver, "You're important to me, so I took the time to make this gift look lovely for you." It leads the receiver to believe that underneath all the wrapping is something to be valued.

All human beings are a gift to the people around them. As wives we are a gift to our husbands. Certainly the inner person is the true gift—the heart, character, personality, and soul each of us possesses. I'm so very grateful that 1 Samuel 16:7 assures us, "The LORD does not look at the things man looks at. Man looks at the outward appearance, but the LORD looks at the heart." How wonderful to know that we are deeply loved by God for who we are and not what we look like! Does that mean that our outside wrapping is unimportant? Not at all.

As much as we wish people didn't notice outward appearance, the reality is that humans are designed to have an eye for beauty. That's why we're so refreshed by a beautiful sunset or a lovely work of art. In *Beauty by the Book*, Nancy Stafford writes, "We need beauty in our lives....We are born with a deep longing for and appreciation of beauty. Our spirits are drawn to it. It calls to us, nourishes us, stimulates us."[1]

The Essence of Beauty

Nancy addresses the confusion many of us feel about inward versus outward beauty. Because she felt ugly as a child, her mom was constantly reassuring her, "Nancy, honey, you're so beautiful on the inside. That's what counts." But Nancy couldn't help noticing that people in the world around her often focused on outward beauty—and by their standards, she didn't measure up. She writes today, "What I know most about beauty has come from God healing my heart and showing me who I really am. He has turned the ashes of my life into beauty, the mourning into joy."[2]

Expensive makeup or the perfect haircut cannot change who we are on the inside. Interestingly enough, the opposite is not true. Our spirit on the inside *does* influence how we look on the outside. I'm sure you've seen women who don't have perfect features or wear the latest styles, yet they have a beauty about them that radiates from an inner glow. You've also seen outwardly lovely people who, with one snide comment or snarled look, ruin their image of pseudo beauty.

The apostle Peter recognized the importance of a women's inner beauty when he said, "Your beauty should not come from outward adornment, such as braided hair and the wearing of gold jewelry and fine clothes. Instead, it should be that of your inner self, the unfading beauty of a gentle and quiet spirit, which is of great worth in God's sight" (1 Peter 3:3–4). Was Peter telling us to forget completely about outward beauty? No, he was telling us not to be dependent upon the outward appearance, because it is the lovely spirit within us that really makes us beautiful.

The noble wife in Proverbs 31 dressed nicely in "fine linen and purple" (v. 22). Yet her true beauty came from her devotion to God, as we read in verse 30: "Charm is deceptive, and beauty is fleeting; but a woman who fears the LORD is to be praised." The essence of our beauty ought to come from the lovely inner qualities of our lives as godly women. Outer beauty is simply giftwrapping.

Several weeks ago Curt called me from work and asked how my writing was going. At the time I was writing the chapter on respect, so I asked him if he had any thoughts on practical ways women could show respect to their husbands. Curt answered with complete conviction, "One way women can show respect for their husbands is to look nice for them." He went on to explain that husbands feel valued and respected when they know their wives have taken time and made a special effort to look their best for them. His comment made me think again about the value of giftwrapping. What's inside is most important, but the effort we put into wrapping the gift shows the recipient we really care.

Curt felt strongly about this point. He told me that while a husband might *say* he doesn't care about his wife's appearance, most men really do. Men are visual. They are stimulated by what they see.

OK, OK. I don't like it either. Looking our best takes work, and who wants to put so much effort into fixing up the outside when it's the inside that counts, right? Let's be honest. Outward appearance isn't the main thing, but it is *something*. The real gift we give our husbands is a loving, respectful, godly spirit. But a gift of such value really ought to be wrapped nicely, don't you think?

Our husbands aren't the only ones who will benefit. When we take care of ourselves and make the effort to look our best, *we* feel better. We're more confident and assured. The key is to keep a balanced perspective.

Can Everyone Be Beautiful?

Isn't it fun to watch those television shows that take seemingly homely women and do complete makeovers on them? New hairstyle, new clothes, new makeup—new look! After the makeover is complete, the women walk out on stage with big smiles and new confidence. That brings me to the question: Does everyone have the potential to look attractive? Or is beauty only possible for those who are born with naturally beautiful features?

Marilyn Vos Savant (the lady known for having the highest IQ) was asked this very question in her column, "Ask Marilyn," in *Parade* magazine. Her response was encouraging and honest. She said that "looks" include everything about your appearance—"the manner in which you smile, the way you wear your hair, the sort of clothing you choose, the body you've developed (through exercise and eating habits), the style of your bearing, and the way you've learned to speak." Most people's appeal is based on their entire "look" and not simply their "beautiful faces," she said. Presence, not facial beauty, is what counts.

She concluded her article with this advice: Instead of growing bitter over the fact that people may judge you based on your appearance, get actively involved in doing what you can do to improve yourself. "Good looks are much more a matter of choice than you realize," she added.[3]

In the following section we will look at some of the ways we can improve our outside packaging. As we do, let's not lose sight of the fact that the greatest beauty of all is the beauty that radiates from within. A godly, gracious, loving, honest, and positive woman offers an unsurpassed gift of loveliness to her spouse and the people around her. In chapters 16 and 17, we will discuss in depth the value of spiritual beauty, strength, and vitality. For now let's agree that the time we spend on making the outward appearance beautiful should pale in comparison to the time we spend developing our inner beauty. And how do we develop inner beauty? By spending time with God on a daily basis. Our devotional time releases the potent beautifiers of love, joy, peace, patience, kindness, goodness, faithfulness, gentleness, and self-control. It's the most important part of our daily beauty routine.

The Beautiful Package

First Corinthians 6:19–20 says, "Do you not know that your body is a temple of the Holy Spirit, who is in you, whom you have received from God? You are not your own; you were bought at a price. Therefore honor God with your body." When you make an effort to look and feel your best, you show that you value the body God has given you to house his Spirit. Here are some areas to consider as you care for your body and develop a beautification plan.

Get exercise.

The mere mention of the word *exercise* brings a smile to your face, I'm sure! Or was that a grimace? Honestly, exercise can be a smiling

There is no cosmetic for beauty like happiness. —Lady Blessington matter if you find an exercise program that suits you. I am amazed at how much better I feel physically, mentally, and emotionally after a hearty workout. Studies show that exercise increases the endorphins (the feel-good hormones) in the brain, producing a natural emotional lift. It increases the flow of blood and oxygen to the brain cells. I don't know about you, but my brain cells need all the help they can get! In addition, working out leaves us with a healthy glow and, if done regularly, results in better muscle tone and a sleeker physique (the foremost reason most women start an exercise routine).

Choose an activity you enjoy. My daughter just discovered kick boxing. Although it's a grueling workout, she loves it and looks forward to going to her kick-boxing classes several times a week. My other daughter loves running and has joined her school's cross-country team, which runs at 6:00 each morning. You have to enjoy running (at least a little) to have that kind of commitment!

What about you? What can you see yourself doing? I suggest planning a workout routine that you can do at least three times a week. Don't use lack of time as an excuse; you can begin with short, thirty-minute workouts. Make it easy on yourself. You don't have to join a health club if it's inconvenient or cost prohibitive. Walk in your neighborhood or through a local mall. Ask your spouse or a friend to join you. Rent or purchase a workout video. Take an inexpensive aerobics class at your local community center. Do floor exercises before you go to bed at night. So many options are at your disposal! The key is to pick one, get started, and just do it.

Eat well.

Recently on one of Curt's convention trips to Europe, We made a profound observation: Generally speaking, French people seem physically trim. And generally speaking, Americans are not. As Curt and I sat at an outdoor café and watched people walk by, we had no difficulty picking out the Americans, because many of them were overweight.

Why are the French people thinner? we wondered. We came up with three reasons. One, they walk everywhere. (There's that exercise thing again.) Two, they eat slowly, savoring their food. Americans have a quick-eat and gotta-go mentality; Europeans linger and enjoy their meals. Many times, after finishing a wonderful dinner at one of the fine restaurants in Europe, we nearly had to attack our waiter to get him to give us our bill!

Third, the French eat more natural, nonprocessed foods. Eating highly processed food is perhaps our biggest downfall in America. William T. Clower, a neurophysiologist at the University of Pittsburgh, wrote a diet book specifically about the French way of eating. In *The Fat Fallacy: Applying the French Diet to the American Lifestyle,* he notes that many of the diet foods we eat today are "faux foods." The wisest way to eat is to choose whole foods and then eat them slowly. Take smaller bites, and chew each one completely. Since it takes twenty minutes for the stomach to signal to the brain that it is full, gulping down meals only promotes overeating.[4] (Why didn't Curt and I take our observations of the French and write our own diet book?)

Gary Smalley, in his book *Food and Love,* warns against four foods or food categories that are bad for our emotional or physical health: white or refined sugar, white or refined flour, hydrogenated oils (and animal fat), and chemically laden foods.[5] You may be thinking, *But don't the French eat those foods sometimes?* Well, yes, but not nearly to the extent that Americans do. And that brings me to my final point on eating well. Contradictions abound in the diet world, but the benefits of eating more whole foods (unprocessed foods), eating slowly, and eating smaller portions can't be disputed. Remember that food is the fuel for your body. Put in the "high-octane"—whole, nutritious food—for more energy and better health!

Update your hairstyle.

It's easy to get in the hairstyle rut. Early in our adult lives, most of us find a hairdo that we can work with, and we keep it forever. It may not be the perfect style for us. It may not even be in style. But we're comfortable with it, and we don't want to change. Granted, having a "do" that's easy to work with is helpful, considering the fast pace of our lives. But now and then we need to consider an update.

Your hairdo is what people notice first when they look at you. It frames your face, so choosing the best cut for your facial features is important. When was the last time you asked your hairdresser what he or she thinks would look great on you? Most hairdressers are trained to distinguish the best hairstyles for various face shapes. Ask a few friends who seem to have an eye for style to give you their opinions too.

There are a few classic cuts, but most hairstyles go in and out with the times. One lady I know wore a beehive hairdo for years. Finally she decided to get her hair cut differently, and the result was fantastic—she looked like a whole new woman! She asked her friends later, "Why didn't you tell me how awful my hair looked?" They replied, "You never asked." Go ahead, be brave and ask!

Update your makeup.

I like to use the term "beauty enhancer" when I talk about makeup. That's what makeup really is: a tool to enhance and draw out your God-given beauty. It's not meant to alter your look completely. How should you wear your makeup? I can't say, because I can't see your face right now. But there are many people who can help you find your best look. Visit any makeup counter at a department store, or ask a local makeup consultant (for Avon or Mary Kay, for example) to come to your home and do free makeovers for you and your friends. Reexamine your makeup routine from time to time and stay current.

While we're focused on faces, I want to mention how important it is to take care of our skin as we age. A gentle cleanser and a good moisturizer are valuable tools for keeping your face looking fresh and youthful. Have you ever considered getting a facial? Wouldn't that make a good birthday gift to yourself? Remember, your face is the part of you that most clearly reflects your heart, so take good care of it!

Don't forget to smile.

You probably think I represent the Smile Brigade by the way I talk so often about smiles. But I truly believe a smile is one of the best ways we can express the joy God has placed within us. A smile can take a so-so looking woman and infuse her with great beauty. Certainly we can't smile all of the time; there are times to mourn and be solemn. But let's not miss opportunities to enhance our beauty with a glowing smile when we can. Recently my friend's daughter competed in the Miss Texas pageant. Do you think any of those girls walked down the center aisle with a frown or a neutral expression? No way—every girl had the biggest, boldest, most bodacious smile on her face! These young ladies were in a beauty contest, and they knew how much a smile would enhance their beauty.

Of course, you and I aren't in a beauty contest. But we can make the best possible presentation of ourselves by simply adding a smile—not a fake smile, but one that says, "I have joy in my heart, and I want to share it with you." You'll find that the joy you bring to others through your smile will give *you* an incredible lift too. Don't forget this most important beauty tool!

Check your wardrobe.

You don't have to spend a lot of money on clothes to look your best. In fact, the key to a good wardrobe is not having more clothes, but having the right clothes. I've noticed, for example, that every time I wear royal blue, people tell me I look great. They say the color brings out my eyes. Big signal! When I shop, I need to focus on a few good royal blue shirts or outfits. To find *your* best colors, hold up different colored outfits as you stand in front of a mirror and see which ones make you "come alive." Ask friends what they think. Even your husband may have an opinion on this one.

Style is another matter. Often we see an outfit in a magazine or on a friend and assume it would look good on us. Not necessarily! Know your own style. What fits your personality? Are you conservative, classic, romantic, earthy? Suit yourself—literally. Investigate new looks, fads, and styles, but always consider what looks right on you.

I highly recommend doing a closet overhaul. We tend to wear 20 percent of our clothes 80 percent of the time, so weed out what you don't wear and get rid of all the clothes that don't look best on you. Give them to charity or a friend or sister. Now you have room in your closet for your best looks, and you are not distracted by clothes clutter. Shop carefully for good buys that look great. Focus on solid colors and accessorize with jewelry and belts to add flair. If money is an issue, shop at outlets and discount stores (my favorites); but don't fall into the trap I often do of buying something just because it is on sale.

One last thought on clothing. Some husbands have an opinion about what they would enjoy seeing their wives wear. Ask your spouse if he has any preferences and give him an opportunity to provide input. He may surprise you with his good taste.

The Comparison Trap

Can I be honest with you? I have always struggled with the beauty issue and comparing myself with others. As a young girl, I didn't feel

He has made everything beautiful in its time. He has also set eternity in the hearts of men; yet they cannot fathom what God has done from beginning to end. —Ecclesiastes 3:11

pretty. Maybe it was because the boys in sixth grade made fun of my oversized nose. Maybe it was because I wasn't a "beauty queen" in high school. Maybe it was due to my own lack of self-confidence. Today my facial features are still not symmetrical, my body is not perfectly proportioned, and my thighs have dimples. When I think about being beautiful, I look at all the beautiful people around me and begin to fret. It is easy to fall into the comparison trap even to this day.

The problem with comparing ourselves to others is that there will always be people who are prettier than us, and there will always be people who are uglier than us. Our goal is not to look more beautiful than the next girl, but rather to look our best by taking care of ourselves. My message in this chapter is not intended to drive us to an inordinate focus on looks. My goal is to make us think about offering our husbands the giftwrapping of an attractive appearance. While we ought to be deliberate about looking our best, the fact remains that our appearance is simply the wrapping paper leading to the valuable gift of a godly woman inside.

These days I try to avoid comparison completely. When it rears its head, I remind myself of its detrimental effects and dismiss it from my mind. Each morning, as I get ready for the day ahead, I do the best I can with what God has given me—starting with a conscious choice to walk with him. As I take that final look in the mirror and walk out the door, I determine to forget about myself and focus on how I can love and serve others.

While we may act ugly or have an ugly attitude, we were not created ugly. We were created by design. God lovingly and perfectly fashioned us just as he wanted us. May we see that God-given beauty not only in ourselves, but also in every human being! Dear sister, don't waste another moment comparing yourself to others. Stand confidently in the knowledge that God has made you in his image and fashioned you for a purpose. All the fluff you do on the outside simply enhances the beauty already inherent in you, because you are his creation. The true essence of a lovely appearance radiates from the inside out.

Allow me to close with a poem by my friend Anne Peters. Anne is a beautiful person, both inside and out. She has seen much pain and heartache in her life; but through it all, she continues to find her hope and strength in Christ. I close with her poem "Beats the Heart of Beauty." I hope it is a gift and a blessing to you.

Lord I come before You
With this gentle plea
Show me all the beauty
That lives inside of me
May it start to blossom
As a rose born from a bud
May it come to shine forth
By the wonders of Your love
I pray to see its splendor
In the way I move and speak
A gentle loving spirit
True beauty that I seek
No perfume made of orchids
No jewels or precious gold
Can replace the joyful beauty
My heart does long to hold
May I know both joy and faith
And clothe myself with peace
And wear the crown of beauty
That Jesus gave to me
For in the promise love has shared

"The two shall be as one"

Beats the heart of beauty

In perfect unison

Oh, Lord I come before you

With this gentle plea

Please show me all the beauty

That lives inside of me

POWER POINT

⚙ **Read:** Song of Songs (also called Song of Solomon) chapters 1–4. Notice the emphasis Solomon and his bride place on enjoying one another's beauty. What are some of the terms they use repeatedly to describe each other? Now turn to Psalm 139:13–16 and relish the reminder that you are a "designer original."

♡ **Pray:** Oh, glorious Creator, Designer, and Savior, you are the source of all that's beautiful in this world! With your creative hand, you have fashioned me just the way you want me. You have a plan and a purpose for my life. Help me to be lovely both inside and out. Show me ways I can enhance my outward appearance as a gift to my husband. More importantly, help me abide in your presence all day long so your Spirit can produce in me the beautiful inner qualities of love, joy, peace, patience, kindness, goodness, faithfulness, gentleness, and self-control. In Jesus' name I pray, amen.

♀ **Remember:** "Charm is deceptive, and beauty is fleeting; but a woman who fears the LORD is to be praised" (Proverbs 31:30).

☺ **Do:** Stand in front of a mirror and take a moment to evaluate your "wrapping." Are there any changes you want to make? Consider a new hairstyle or cosmetics makeover. What about a new exercise routine or better eating habits? Take a look at your wardrobe and weed out a few "oldies." If your budget allows, shop for a new outfit in a color and style that looks best on you.

Now take a look in the mirror of God's Word by reading Galatians 5:22–23. Do you reflect the beauty of a godly spirit in your attitude and actions? Determine to enhance your beauty by spending time with God each day through prayer and feeding on his Word.

13

Sensational Sex
How to Be a Great Lover

God gave the gift of sex like a precious jewel to humanity—
the crown of all His creation.

—William Fitch

"Sexual Pleasure Crash Course—Satisfaction Guaranteed for Every Reader."

Caught your attention, didn't I? Lest you think those are my words and that's my guarantee for this chapter, I must tell you that I saw that title on the cover of a popular women's magazine. Other magazines in the rack boasted these articles:

"Taboo Sex: The Eight Secrets Every Woman Must Try."

"The Shy Girl's Guide to Sex"

"Get Him Hot—Eight Naughty Dares to Try with Your Man Tonight"

Take a look at the magazines in the checkout aisle at most grocery stores, and you get an eyeful of erotic titles! Let's face it: In today's society, sex sells. Articles encouraging moments of illicit passion abound, but books encouraging Christian women to enjoy the fullness of sex with their husbands in marriage are far and few between. In church circles, sex is not a common topic of conversation. "Good girls don't" was about the sum of the sexual advice we received in our dating years. I think it's time to break the ice and address the topic of sex with a fresh and balanced perspective, don't you?

God intentionally designed sexuality. The act of sexual intimacy is a picture of the oneness he designed for us to experience in marriage. Between a husband and wife, sexual intimacy is holy and wonderful. It's a blessed gift and a vital part of a healthy marriage relationship. We're meant to enjoy it to the fullest! H. Norman Wright and Wes Roberts, authors of *Before You Say "I Do,"* explain, "In the plan of God, sex was intended to provide a means of totally revealing oneself to the beloved, of pouring one's energies and deepest affection, hopes, and dreams into the loved one."[1] Lovemaking enriches and deepens the commitment and communion between a man and a woman who've given themselves to one another in marriage.

What Sex Is and What It's Not

Sex is not just a physical act. *Yeah, right. Tell that to a man,* you may be thinking. But in his book *Becoming a Couple of Promise,* Dr. Kevin Leman says that even men don't just want sex; they want "sexual fulfillment," and there is a distinct difference. "Fulfillment comes in the exploration and enjoyment of our sexual *complementarities,*" Leman says. "For a man, this involves feeling completely accepted by his wife....She loves him with all of his fears, flaws, and foibles. She perfectly accepts his ways of loving and lets him know that he is the greatest. Then his enjoyment is complete."[2] Sex is more than an activity; it is a pleasurable, encouraging, and fulfilling experience.

The intimacy of sex is deeply rooted in our beings—a binding together of two people in the deepest sense. By God's design, Genesis 2:22–24 tells us, a man leaves his father and mother and unites with his wife, and the two become "one flesh." Sexual union has great significance in God's plan for marriage. That's why Paul gave this stern warning against immorality in 1 Corinthians 6:15–16: "Do you not know that your bodies are members of Christ himself? Shall I then take the members of Christ and unite them with a prostitute? Never! Do you not know that he who unites himself with a prostitute is one with her in body?"

Sex is the most intimate form of unity, and it is reserved for those who are committed to one another in marriage. Paul speaks about the topic of marital sex in 1 Corinthians 7:

> The husband should fulfill his marital duty to his wife, and likewise the wife to her husband. The wife's body does not belong to her alone but also to her husband. In the same way, the husband's body does not belong to him alone but also to his wife. Do not deprive each other except by mutual consent and for a time, so that you may devote yourselves to prayer. Then come together again so that Satan will not tempt you because of your lack of self-control. I say this as a concession, not as a command. (vv. 3–6)

In this passage we're reminded that sexual intimacy is a giving of ourselves to our spouses. We don't belong solely to ourselves; we also belong to our husbands, and they belong to us. Sex is not a reward—something we can give or withhold in order to control, manipulate, or show our husbands we are hurt about something (as some wives have been known to do). Scripture is clear that sex must not be used that way. In the Amplified Bible, the word *deprive* in verse 5 is expanded to include the words *refuse* and *defraud*. We must not refuse, deprive, or defraud our husbands of sexual intimacy except in times of focused prayer—and then only by mutual consent and for a limited period of time. As William Fitch said, "In all fully Christian marriages, there should be the full enjoyment of sex as God gave it and as He meant it to be enjoyed. To deny it is to deny a gift that has capacities for untold good."[3]

As we've said before, the union of a husband and wife in marriage is a reflection of the relationship between Christ and the church. Ephesians 5:28–32 tells us:

> In this same way, husbands ought to love their wives as their own bodies. He who loves his wife loves himself. After all, no one ever hated his own body, but he feeds and cares for it, just as Christ does the church—for we are members of his body. "For this reason a man will leave his father and mother and be united to his wife, and the two will become one flesh." This is a profound mystery—but I am talking about Christ and the church.

In a way that is as beautiful as it is mysterious, married love is a picture of the love that Christ has for his church—and that's you and me. Evangelist and author Jack Taylor explains it like this: "The deep spiritual significance of sex speaks of the fellowship between Christ and his church. There is deep expression, communication, and satisfaction in this fellowship."[4] May we never take our sexual union with our husbands for granted! God uses the marriage relationship as an image of our relationship with Christ. That means it must be honored, respected, preserved, and enjoyed.

Focusing on One Another

The media bombards us with images of men and women interested in pursuing their own sexual pleasures. But most women don't have sex for mere pleasure alone. In fact, many women find it difficult to experience pleasure consistently. The good news is that married women are more apt to enjoy sex. Why? Because typically it takes time, effort, and communication for females to experience pleasure in sex—and these qualities are most likely to be developed in marriage. Husbands and wives who've made a lifetime commitment can focus on one another's pleasure and not just their own.

It is interesting to read the romantic exchanges between Solomon and the Shulammite woman in Song of Songs and notice that the lovers are not focused on themselves but on one another. Solomon is completely consumed with his lover, praising her, hoping for her pleasure, and wanting only the best for her. The Shulammite woman has the same feelings and intentions toward him. What this tells us is that sex is not a matter of looking for what we can get; it's looking for what we can give. A healthy sexual relationship involves a wife pouring herself out for the pleasure of her husband. And one of the ways a husband receives pleasure is by giving his wife pleasure.

The way the two lovers in Song of Songs communicate intimately with one another sets a good example for us in our marriages. Men and women have different needs, desires, and expectations about sex; that's a given. So how will we know what our husbands desire, and how will they know what we desire, unless we communicate on an intimate level?

I know. Conveying thoughts and feelings about sex isn't always easy. Both husbands and wives find it difficult to identify and verbalize what pleases them sometimes. As marriage experts David and Claudia Arp say, "It takes time to communicate, to work through conflict, and to build a creative love life."[5]

When you talk about sex with your husband, make sure both of you are comfortable with the time, place, and conversation. Be gentle and patient in your discovery of one another's likes and dislikes. Look for opportunities to say, "I like that," or, "Does that feel good to you?" You can communicate with words, sounds, or touch to convey your thoughts. You'll learn best by doing, experimenting, and experiencing— and communicating openly during the process.

Sex provides a means of presenting one's spouse with the gift of oneself and experiencing a like gift in return.
—H. Norman Wright and Wes Roberts

Allow me to add a brief side note here. Some women have an especially hard time desiring sex. This could be due to physical challenges, relationship problems, or personal issues from the past. If you find yourself in this situation, talk to your doctor about any health-related issues and consider seeing a (female) Christian counselor who can help you uncover and deal with any emotional or relational barriers to intimacy.

Sex at Any Age

Communication throughout marriage is important, because a sexual relationship is not a static thing. It changes naturally over the years. But sex can still be great at any age!

Generally speaking, during our newlywed years we are young, passionate, and energetic. This is a wonderful time of exploration and learning new things about our spouses. Assuming children are not yet involved, we have our mornings and evenings alone together without the interruption of kids; and that gives us a unique and special opportunity to focus on getting to know one another's bodies, likes, and dislikes. These early years of marriage are a growth time for the relationship—physically, mentally, emotionally, and spiritually.

As we get a little older (say, in our midthirties), life gets busy. As wives we are often physically exhausted from taking care of the kids and the home and perhaps working outside the home. At this stage in the game, our sex lives may become somewhat routine, although we can be quite content. We may not have the mad passion of the early years, but we (and our spouses) can experience an enriching and satisfying love life if we'll continue to communicate and understand each other's needs and desires. (Important note: With children in the house, a lock on the bedroom door is highly recommended.)

Oddly enough, experts say the midthirties is when women reach their "sexual stride." Don't you wonder about the timing? Comedian Rita Rudner says jokingly, "Men reach their sexual peak at eighteen. Women reach their sexual peak at thirty-five. Do you get the feeling God is into practical jokes? We're reaching our sexual peak right around the same time they're discovering they have a favorite chair."[6]

In our thirties and forties, we often feel more confident about ourselves and our lives. We recognize what we enjoy, and we're more comfortable expressing our desires. Staying close and connected with our husbands through this stage helps us increase enjoyment in the bedroom. We need to be deliberate about paying attention to our mates and make it a priority to find time for intimate moments with them. Sex may need to be a little more planned or scheduled; but it can be great—especially if we build the anticipation for it all day long (see the "Creative Lover" section that follows shortly).

As we grow older (or let's just say, as we *mature*), our hormone levels decrease and our bodies may not respond exactly like they used to—but that doesn't mean we can't maintain vibrant sex lives. The good news is that we don't have as many distractions at this stage of life. Our kids are older and perhaps out on their own. We know our husbands better. We know what they like and how to satisfy and fulfill them, and they know the same about us.

We also know other ways to communicate our love. "When you're young, you demonstrate love more often with sex," says one happily married, seventy-seven-year-old Michigan husband responding to a marriage survey. "But when you're older, you find there are many other ways—a peck on the back or the neck or a pat on the butt."[7] Couples need to leave room for continual learning and understanding. Yes, aging can have an effect on sex drive and performance. But we can find positive ways to change along with these things and still maintain happy love lives.

Creative Lover

Whatever stage of life we're in, we need to continually look for ways to add a new spark of excitement and avoid ruts. Linda Dillow, author of *Creative Counterpart,* says this: "The woman who would never think of serving her husband the same microwave dinner every night sometimes serves him the same sexual response time after time after time. Sex, like supper, loses much of its flavor when it becomes totally predictable."[8] Let's look at some ways we can step out of the ordinary and make our love lives extraordinary.

Try foreplay all day.

Build the interest and anticipation for a late-night delight with your hubby by giving him a few playful hints throughout the day. Yes, you can and should flirt with your husband! Here are some fun ideas to try:

- Write him a short, sexy note letting him know your hopes and intentions for later: "Can't wait for you to get home tonight." "Let's get hot and heavy tonight, handsome." "Let's have some fun after the kids go to bed tonight." Put the note where only he will see it at home, or sneak it into his briefcase or pocket. Warning: Do be careful that the note doesn't get into the wrong hands! I know a woman who wrote a sexy note to her husband on the back of what she thought was one of her child's old school papers. It was actually a homework assignment that had to be turned in the next day. The child came home from school with a note from the teacher saying, "I thought you might want this note back—and next time be careful where you write a note to your husband!"

- Touch him or rub his back. Get to know how he likes to be touched, and look for the right timing. A soft, sexy, flirtatious touch can build the mood and give the nonverbal cue that you are looking forward to later.

- Write a note on your bathroom mirror using a dry-erase marker. Tell him you are looking forward to a "hot and steamy" time tonight. Add a lipstick impression of your lips. (Yes, kiss the mirror after you have applied an abundance of lipstick!)

- Call him at the office and, using a soft, sexy voice, tell him you are looking forward to his coming home from work. Make sure he is not on speakerphone!

- Cuddle with him while you are still in bed in the morning. Let him know your hopeful intentions for that evening. Tell him you will be looking forward to your special time together all through the day.

- Prepare a romantic candlelight dinner. (If you have kids, send them to Grandma's house or arrange for them to spend the evening with friends.) The room should be dimly lit with romantic music playing in the background. Look into his eyes, listen to him, and don't talk about the cares of the day or the children's activities. Smile and enjoy each other's company.

Make a bedroom fashion statement.

Don't spend your entire fashion budget on the clothes that everyone sees. Set at least a little money aside for what only your husband will see. I make a point of purchasing new, sexy sleepwear whenever we are planning to go on a trip without the kids. I also use a little of my birthday and Christmas money for new nightgowns or teddies. You don't need a large budget to look great in the bedroom, I promise. I do much of my shopping for appealing apparel at discount and outlet stores.

It's easy to get into a fashion slump when it comes to PJ apparel.

Why? Because everyone wants to go to sleep in something comfortable. But while your favorite flannel gown may be great for a cold winter night, you also need to invest in some terrific teddies too. Fortunately, being sexy doesn't necessarily mean being uncomfortable. Visit the lingerie department at your favorite store and look for something that has both sex appeal and comfort. The two can coexist, trust me. Of course, now and then you may want to buy one of those totally impractical little numbers!

I'm not suggesting that you try to look like a Frederick's of Hollywood model. I'm just encouraging you to put some effort into looking fresh and appealing in the bedroom. The point is to show your husband that he is so important to you that you want to look attractive for him.

Use variety to make it fun.

Sex within the bonds of marriage is a wonderful thing. Spice it up with some variety, and have fun! Light candles all around the room before you turn out the lights. Purchase massage oil and give each other a body massage. Take a bubble bath together. Step into the shower sometime when he is taking his morning shower.

If the kids are away, consider smooching and making love on the living-room sofa (or in the kitchen, or on the rug in the hallway, or…). Try new places for your sexual rendezvous. You may want to talk intimately sometime about what you would enjoy together so that the next time the kids are away, you're ready for action.

Enjoy!

One of my new favorite movies is *My Big Fat Greek Wedding*. Have you seen it? It's a hilarious portrayal of Greek tradition in a large Greek-American family. I'll never forget the scene when the entire female population of the bride's family is helping her get ready for the ceremony. In walk her excited mom and flamboyant aunt, who sit the bride down on the edge of the bed to have "The Talk." The mother's words of wisdom come down to this: "Greek women are lambs in the kitchen, but they are tigers in the bedroom."

Go ahead, be a tiger! Enjoy the blessings, pleasures, and benefits of a fulfilling marriage and an intimate sex life. As you and your husband grow in your love for one another, your sex life can't help but flourish.

I think of the story told by C. H. Parkhurst in his book *Love as a Lubricant.* (Don't get any funny ideas from the title; this is actually a very old book on the topic of Christian love). A workman boarded a trolley one day and sat down. Upon noticing that the trolley door squeaked every time it opened, he got up from his seat, pulled out a little can from his pocket, and put a drop of oil on the offending spot. As he sat down again, he quietly remarked, "I always carry an oil can in my pocket, for there are so many squeaky things that a drop of oil will correct."

Parkhurst concludes the story with this point: "Love is the oil which alone can make everyday life in home and business and society harmonious."[9] He's right. And when it comes to sex in particular, love is the oil that covers the challenges, frustrations, and any feelings of inadequacy we might have in the bedroom. In fact, someone ought to write a how-to book entitled *Love Each Other to Better Sex.* Love is a giving of ourselves unconditionally to another. It's consummated in marriage in the beautiful and selfless act of sex between husband and wife.

Allow me to give one word of warning before we close: Intimacy is meant to be shared with your mate only. In today's world, sad to say, the number of wives leaving their husbands due to affairs with other men is on the rise. Don't be naive. Guard your eyes, your heart, and your actions. Don't destroy your marriage for the false hope that someone else has something better to offer. What God has joined together, let no woman put asunder! Watch how you dress, how you act, and what you say to other men. Sex and romance must be shared with your husband and no one else.

The very best sex takes place between two people who have committed their lives to one another, who love each other so much that they only seek each other's pleasure. So enjoy your husband. Enjoy your sex life. As a positive wife, let your intimacy flow out of a heart full of love for that special one who said, "I do."

POWER POINT

⚙ **Read:** Song of Songs chapters 5–8. What do you notice about the way the two lovers communicate with one another? What indications of selfless love do you glean from this reading? How can you be more like the Shulammite bride in your marriage?

♡ **Pray:** Glorious Lord and perfect Savior, I am overwhelmed by your abundant love for me! I worship and adore you as the marvelous Creator of the universe and loving heavenly Father to your people. Thank you for my husband and for the beautiful gift of sex that you have given us in marriage. Help me to faithfully love and enjoy my husband all the days of our lives. Show me how to be his mate, his helper, his lover, and his friend. Help me to selflessly and completely love him, and help him to love me the same way. In Jesus' name I pray, amen.

♀ **Remember:** "My lover is mine, and I am his" (Song of Solomon 2:16 NLT).

☺ **Do:** Plan a romantic night at home with your husband. (Make arrangements for the kids to be at Grandma's or a friend's house.) Begin the day by hinting to him about the pleasure that is to come. Use some of the ideas from this chapter or create your own romantic adventure, keeping in mind what you know he would enjoy.

Power Principle #6

THe
Power
oF
Responsibility

Be sure to do what you should, for then you will enjoy the personal satisfaction of having done your work well, and you won't need to compare yourself to anyone else. For we are each responsible for our own conduct.

—Galatians 6:4–5 NLT

There are no shortcuts to any place worth going.

—Beverly Sills

Yours, Mine, and Ours
Fun with Finances 101

There is no dignity quite so impressive, and no independence quite so important, as living within your means.

—Calvin Coolidge

Shelley was thrilled to finally live in a decent neighborhood. For years her husband had jumped from one job to another, which meant they never had enough money for a down payment on a house, much less a stable income for a mortgage. But then Steve found the "job of his dreams," and they decided they were ready to take the plunge. They knew the monthly mortgage payments would be a stretch, but they were willing to cut back in other areas to make their dream work. Finally they had a house with a yard!

It didn't take long after moving into their new home to meet the neighbors. Soon they were going to weekend barbeques and eating out at local restaurants with their newfound acquaintances. Shelley noticed that when they got together, the other women were always wearing cute, new outfits. She felt a little frumpy next to them, so she figured a trip to the mall was just the solution. She came home that afternoon with just a few purchases to update her wardrobe.

One night after having dinner at the Wilsons' next door, Steve commented, "Wasn't their home decorated nicely?" Taking the hint, Shelley went to Home Expo the very next day to pick up a few things to spruce up the house. Meanwhile Steve began to notice that everyone in the neighborhood took great pride in their yards. When he looked at the landscaping around his own house, he was a little embarrassed. Not a problem—a quick trip to the local nursery and a weekend working in the yard brought their home up to snuff.

Steve enjoyed his new job. He was making more money than ever before, so he figured it was time to get a new car. It was a business necessity, after all; not only would it be a reflection of his success, but it would speak volumes to his clients. So he went down to the car lot, chose the perfect luxury car for his needs, and started the monthly payments. Around the same time, Shelley discovered that she could buy her groceries on credit in order to defer the payment for a while. Using the card was a matter of convenience; and besides, she received advantage points every time she used it. It sure came in handy when she wanted to buy that stylish coat for the fall.

When the blessing and joy of children came along, so did the increased expenses of diapers, food, and clothing—not to mention the burden of paying the rest of the hospital bill. (Insurance didn't cover as much as they had expected.) A new, kid-friendly minivan soon followed. And before they knew it—how could it happen so quickly?—Shelley and Steve found themselves in serious debt, with no savings and no ability to plan for the future.

Sadly, Shelley and Steve are not alone in their financial woes. You know as well as I do that the scenario I just described is all too common. Getting into deep debt can happen so easily! Yet few things strain a marriage more than money problems. According to Mary Stark, author of *What No One Tells the Bride,* more than half of all marital conflicts leading to divorce have to do with finances. She notes that a survey conducted by Citibank showed that "fifty-seven percent of divorced couples cite financial disputes as the primary reason they didn't get along."[1] Fifty-seven percent! Perhaps you read the title of this chapter and said to yourself, *What's money got to do with being a positive wife?* I think that statistic says it all.

As positive wives we want to make sure that money is a tool we use wisely to build a solid foundation and a secure future for our families. We don't want unwise financial decisions to wreck the peace in our marriages and undercut our future plans. But how can we avoid debt, live successfully within our means, and plan for the future too? That's what this chapter is all about.

The bad news is I'm not a financial whiz. The good news is my husband is a certified financial planner who helps people develop sensible, systematic financial strategies that plan for the present and build for the future. When it comes to financial responsibility, he's brilliant! He's the one who provided most of the information for this chapter; I just helped it fall into place on the pages. (He can't type very well.)

In this chapter I'm going to share a number of sound financial strategies that have worked for many, many families over the years. These tried-and-true principles will set you on the path toward financial responsibility. Couples who've followed these principles have found that they are able to organize their income in such a way as to live in the present, save for the future, and still have enough to give to their churches and other nonprofit organizations.

Please understand that the strategies I'm about to share are offered as suggestions only. Use the information as points of discussion with your husband, then work together to make the financial decisions that are best for you.

Every couple is different. In some families, the wife is the keeper of the finances; in others, the husband is; and in many, money matters are handled equally by both spouses. Whatever way you choose, you must have a workable strategy. A word of caution: If you're not the one who handles the finances in your home, please don't nag your husband about these ideas! My intent here is to offer some basic principles and a few thoughts for you to consider. Discuss them with your husband in a spirit of harmony, not discord.

Contentment Is Great Gain

The foundational principle I want to start with doesn't have to do with money at all; it has to do with the heart. In today's materialistic world, we are encouraged to have many "wants." Sometimes we confuse those wants with needs. We see something; we want it; we think we must have it (even if our checkbooks disagree). As positive wives, let's not get caught in the trap of always wanting more, more, more! Instead, let's ask God to help us develop hearts of contentment. Being content doesn't mean that we never fulfill our wants from time to time; rather, it means that we make our purchasing decisions based on wisdom and sound financial practices, not on emotion or self-indulgence. We maintain a heart of contentment in the midst of all our decision making.

Paul wrote about contentment in his letter to the Philippians. Keep in mind that he was in prison when he penned the following words: "I am not saying this because I am in need, for I have learned to be content whatever the circumstances. I know what it is to be in need, and I know what it is to have plenty. I have learned the secret of being content in any and every situation, whether well fed or hungry, whether living in plenty or in want. I can do everything through him who gives me strength" (Philippians 4:11–13). Now if Paul could make this statement from an awful prison cell, shouldn't we be content in our houses and apartments?

The key to Paul's contentment wasn't a new house or a new couch or a new outfit; it was Christ at work in his life. Paul knew that he could do all things and be content in all circumstances through Christ's strengthening power. Can you say the same? When the budget doesn't allow you to get a new car, can you be content with the old van? When your husband's job doesn't bring in enough income to buy the latest fashions for the kids, can you be content shopping at the discount stores?

Patience is a virtue that goes hand in hand with contentment. We tend to not only want things; we want them *now*. The truth is, we have a greater appreciation for what we buy when we save and wait until we actually have the money for the purchase.

Ultimately the secret of contentment is not in having things; it is in having Christ and allowing him to strengthen us within. Contentment is a matter of what is in the heart, not what is in the hand. Through Christ's strength, when we are tempted to want the here-and-now, we can keep our eyes focused on things of eternal value. It is Christ's power at work in our hearts that helps us overcome the desire for immediate gratification and seek everlasting rewards instead. As Paul told Timothy in 1 Timothy 6:6, "Godliness with contentment is great gain." He went on to warn that the insatiable pursuit of more, more, more will plunge us into "ruin and destruction" (v. 9). May it never be so in our homes!

Establishing a Budget

If our hearts are not right, all the best strategies will be of little use to us. But even as we're asking for God's help to be content, we need to take the practical first step of establishing a workable budget. The following pages give you an example of one way to organize your household budget. You may want to adapt it in a way that works best for you.[2]

Success consists of a series of little daily efforts. —Mamie McCullough

Budget Organizer

Fixed Expenses (Personal)

Fixed Expense Item	Monthly	Annual
Home mortgage		
Property taxes		
Homeowners insurance premium		
Income taxes		
Social security taxes		
Life insurance premiums		
Car payments		
Car insurance payments		
Disability insurance premiums		
Retirement plan contributions		
Club membership dues		
Loan payments (excluding cars and mortgage)		
Medical insurance expenses		
Childcare expenses		
School expenses (tuition and food)		
Other fixed expenses (list)		
Total		

Budget Organizer

Variable Expenses

Variable Expense Item	Monthly	Annual
Utilities (gas, heat, electric, water)		
Telephone		
Clothing		
Laundry and teaching		
Postage		
Doctor and dental		
Charitable contributions		
Auto repair and maintenance		
Auto fuel		
Home repair and maintenance		
Food and toiletries		
Household goods		
Household furnishings		
Savings		
Investments		
Vacations		
Entertainment		
Gifts		
Other variable expenses (list)		
Total		

Budget Organizer

Expenses (Not Paid Monthly)

Non-Monthly Expense Item	Monthly Average	Annual
Tax preparation fee		
Possible retirement plan contributions		
Other annual expenses (list)		
Total		

Fixed and Variable Expenses—Business

Business Expense Item	Monthly Average	Annual
Professional and association dues		
Travel		
Secretarial		
Telephone		
Business entertainment		
Tax and banking services		
Rent/mortgage		
Advertising/promotions		
Postage		
Printing/stationery		
Insurance		
Other (list)		
Total		

After you have devised a budget that is right for your family, you will need to determine the payment methods that you will to use to cover your expenses. You may decide to pay by check for your bills and expenditures; or for convenience, you may want to use automatic draw and debit cards. Some spouses have joint checking accounts, but Curt and I have found that we work best with separate accounts. Curt gives me money from his account (which he uses for business and personal expenses as well as major purchases), and I write out the bills and pay for the groceries from my account. For a while we tried to share a debit card account—until I forgot to tell Curt about a major withdrawal I'd made. Oops! You and your husband will have to determine the system that works best for you. Talk together about the pros and cons of different alternatives and work toward a manageable solution that you can both feel good about.

Creative Ways to Stretch a Dollar

Whatever our family income, most of us have to put a limit on our spending in order to stay within a budget. Fortunately there are many creative ways to stretch a dollar these days. When it comes to shopping, I try to follow two basic rules:

1. Shop sales but only buy what you need.

How many times have you seen something on sale and thought to yourself, *I have to buy it. It's such a great deal!* Recently I stepped into a ladies clothing shop in Austin, Texas, that was advertising a 75 percent off sale. Now that's speaking my language!

But as I entered the store, I could see that it was extremely upscale; even with 75 percent off, the outfits would be expensive.

Then I noticed the ten-dollar rack. According to a sign, everything on the rack was just ten dollars! As I plowed through the clothes, I looked at the original prices. One skirt was originally $600; a simple top was $200; and a silk jacket was $1,750 (yes, you read that right). I was thrilled to spend $30 and purchase $2,550 worth of goods—a savings to our family of $2,520! Isn't that great? Well, yes, except the skirt was neon pink, so I never wore it. The top didn't go with any of my outfits, so I gave it to a friend. I may wear the jacket one day, but so far I haven't found the right occasion. All that to say that sometimes we can get caught up in the "great deal" and end up with things we don't need. Believe me, I know!

2. Shop for quality but always try to get the best price possible.

For clothing, luggage, and home accessories, check the outlet stores (Marshalls, Ross Dress for Less, T. J. Maxx, Horchow, and Tuesday Morning, among others). Don't overlook the discount stores; you may be surprised at what you can find. For furnishings, check out consignment stores, auctions, estate sales, and classified ads in the paper. Just because someone is selling something doesn't mean it's not good quality. Many times you can get a high-quality, barely used item at a fraction of its original cost simply because someone has grown tired of it. This kind of shopping takes time, patience, and a clear idea of what you're looking for. But when you've saved money on a good deal and you have the peace of knowing you've stayed within your budget, the satisfaction is worth the effort.

Systematic Saving and Investing

An important part of any successful budget plan is savings. To prepare adequately for the future, you should look to save or invest at least 10 percent of your gross income (at a minimum). This would include your 401K or other retirement programs at work.

As your first savings priority, create an emergency fund in a money-market or savings account that is equivalent to at least three months of family income. This is for unexpected, emergency expenses—for example, replacing a leaky roof or covering a drop in income after a layoff. Once you have this emergency fund in place, create a separate "put-and-take" account (also in a money-market or savings account) to use for non-everyday, nonemergency expenses that come up periodically, such as vacations, a down payment on a car, or a new kitchen appliance. It's important to keep your "put-and-take" and emergency funds separate; if they're together, you may find it too easy to draw from the emergency fund for nonemergencies. Then you won't have the money you need when a real crisis hits.

Curt has met with hundreds of people over the last twenty years to discuss their finances, and one thing seems to be almost universal: Regardless of income level, people will not save or invest adequately unless they do so systematically. The best way to begin is by setting two savings and investment goals: a minimum and a superior. The first goal is the minimum amount you will put into savings and investments on a monthly basis. The superior goal is the amount over and above the minimum that you can shoot for if your monthly expenses are less than normal or your income is more than you expected. Implement your minimum goal by arranging for a direct deposit to be made from your bank account or payroll check directly into your savings or investment accounts. That will keep you from being tempted to spend the money. When you have extra—say, you get a bonus at work—put that into the account yourself to help achieve your superior goal.

Another kind of investment plan to consider is a college fund for your children. As you probably know, college costs are increasing at a rapid rate. The sooner you can begin investing, the less it will cost you when the time comes for your kids to go off to school. In recent years the government has made it possible for parents and grandparents to invest in their children's college education through excellent tax-advantaged programs called 529 plans. These 529 plans, offered by individual states, allow you to invest money in special mutual funds that will grow tax-deferred and can be withdrawn tax-free if used for college.

Managing Debt

Is it wrong to go into debt for certain items? You'll find a variety of opinions on this subject. Without a doubt, debt is epidemic in our society, and it is the cause of great strain in many families today. But debt is one of those gray areas; I can't give you a cut-and-dry, right-or-wrong answer about it. At the very least, it's something that must be handled wisely and cautiously.

If you're thinking about making a purchase that will put you in debt, my suggestion is that you consider your motive first. What's in your heart? Are you making your decision from a heart of contentment? Prayerfully ask God to reveal to you if any of the following attitudes are at the root of your desire: pride, greed, envy, discontent, covetousness, laziness, self-indulgence, worldliness. If so, repent and ask God to restore a heart of contentment within you. And get out of the store!

Curt typically counsels couples to maintain as little debt as possible. The only debts that may be prudent are mortgage debt, school debt (if you used student loans to pay for college), and possibly a car loan. If you decide to go into debt in one of these areas, make sure that you search for the lowest interest rate possible. Determine a reasonable date for being out of debt and plan to systematically pay down the loan.

Making Mortgage Payments

As we mentioned, a mortgage loan is one kind of debt that many financial counselors consider acceptable. Most mortgage companies figure that you can earmark up to 28 percent of your income for your mortgage payments. A better, more financially sound plan would be to choose a mortgage that consumes no more than 15 to 20 percent of your monthly income. Of course, the cost of housing is higher in certain parts of the country than others, so your geography will have some impact on that percentage. Generally speaking, you should try to go with a fifteen-year mortgage instead of a thirty-year one if at all possible. Fifteen fewer years of mortgage and interest payments add up to significant savings.

The Trouble with Credit Cards

We all know that credit-card debt gets a lot of people into trouble. But in and of themselves, credit cards are not evil. They can be very helpful for certain transactions; for example, when you are renting a car or checking into a hotel. And the wise use of a credit card can help you build up a good credit rating, which is useful when you want to buy a home or make another major purchase.

If you have credit cards, use them only as a convenience—that is, only when you don't have enough cash in your purse and a check is not appropriate. Most importantly, *always pay off your credit-card bills completely each month.* Credit-card companies would love for you to pay only the minimum amount. Why? Because they are charging an enormous rate of interest that builds up their earnings over time. If you spend years paying off your credit cards, all the better for them! If you have significant credit-card debt, consider a consolidation loan, either with a low-interest-rate credit card or with your bank. Determine to make systematic payments in order to pay off your credit cards as quickly as possible.

Risk Management

Sometimes families can be destroyed financially because they haven't made arrangements for proper risk management. What am I talking about? Choosing a good insurance plan. Insurance provides you with peace of mind and helps assure that you won't lose everything if your family is hit with a serious crisis. Most employers provide their employees with some kind of plan for health, disability, and life insurance. However, in most cases these plans only provide a small part of the disability and life-insurance coverage a family really needs.

When it comes to life insurance in particular, many people are grossly underinsured. In order to figure out how much life insurance you need to have on the major breadwinner in your home, follow these steps:

1. Determine how much money your family would need to pay off all debts, including the mortgage, if the major breadwinner were to die.

2. Determine how much money you'd need to send the children to college.

3. Determine the amount of annual income the surviving spouse and children would need in order to maintain their current standard of living. Multiply that annual income by twenty; this dollar amount should be enough to ensure that your family has sufficient assets to invest conservatively for income purposes and to keep pace with inflation (based on an estimated rate of return of 8 percent and a 3 percent inflation rate).

4. Add the numbers from the first three steps, then subtract from that total your current investment and retirement assets. What is left over is the amount of total life insurance you need.

What type of life insurance should you buy? This is another area where you'll find many differing opinions. There are three major types of life insurance—term, whole life, and universal life—with several variations on each type.

Term insurance is initially inexpensive but builds no cash value; in most cases it will expire before the insured person does. Whole life is permanent coverage that builds cash value, will not go up in price, and is designed to be in force no matter when you die. Universal life is a hybrid of term and whole life insurance. Essentially, it is term insurance with a side fund that builds cash value and, if funded properly, can serve as permanent coverage. Both whole life and universal life are much more expensive than term insurance initially; but in many cases, since they build cash value, you can eventually stop paying the premiums and keep the coverage in force. Also, they can be used to help supplement retirement income or to meet other financial needs that may arise.

The type of coverage that's best for your family depends on the length of time you will need the coverage, the amount of coverage you need, and what you can afford. Generally speaking, you should get the amount of life insurance that you need based on the four steps above, and then, if you can afford it, get as much permanent coverage as possible. I encourage you to meet with a good financial planner or insurance agent who can help guide you to the coverage that is best suited for you. He or she can also help you determine if you need additional disability or long-term-care insurance.

A Noble Wife and Her Money

For an example of a positive wife who is responsible with her finances, we can look once again to the noble woman in Proverbs 31. Here is a woman who handles her money in a wise and prudent way. The Amplified Version of the Bible calls her "capable," "intelligent," and "virtuous." Let's close this chapter by gleaning ten lessons from her description in Proverbs 31:11–20:

1. *"Her husband has full confidence in her and lacks nothing of value"* (v. 11). This noble wife is trustworthy with what she is given,

and she handles her responsibilities wisely. What responsibilities are in our hands? Are we handling them in good faith? Can our husbands trust us to stay within a budget?

2. *"She brings him good, not harm, all the days of her life"* (v. 12). We don't want to be the reason our families go into debt. As much as it's in our power to do so, let's do good, not harm, to our financial foundation.

3. *"She selects wool and flax and works with eager hands"* (v. 13). This is a resourceful and ambitious lady. She does what she can to help out. Can the same be said about us?

4. *"She is like the merchant ships, bringing her food from afar"* (v. 14). Apparently she is an enterprising woman who goes to great lengths to get the best deal for her family. Sounds like a good shopper to me.

5. *"She gets up while it is still dark; she provides food for her family and portions for her servant girls"* (v. 15). OK, so she has a maid service. She obviously isn't lazy, but she does have help. When you consider everything else that she does, she probably needs it. Still she gets a jump-start on her day by getting up early; you have to admire her for that.

6. *"She considers a field and buys it; out of her earnings she plants a vineyard"* (v. 16). This noble woman takes part in the financial decisions of the household. She invests her money and receives a good return. Let's consider how we invest our own time and money. Is it profitable?

7. *"She sets about her work vigorously; her arms are strong for her tasks"* (v. 17). She works heartily at the tasks God has given her. What tasks has God given us to do, whether in the home or in

the field? Are we giving our all, or are we going about our work halfheartedly? (Does the last phrase in that verse imply that we need to be lifting weights?)

8. *"She sees that her trading is profitable, and her lamp does not go out at night"* (v. 18). This noble woman is quite astute in her financial decisions. Maybe that kind of money sense comes naturally to her, or maybe she knows enough to seek wise financial counsel. Whatever the case, she makes sure that she makes a profit with her trading. The phrase "her lamp does not go out at night" most likely refers to the fact that by planning ahead and making sound financial decisions, she has the resources to keep the lamps in her house lit at night. In other words, she is confidently prepared. It doesn't mean she stays up all night. We do need our rest!

9. *"In her hand she holds the distaff and grasps the spindle with her fingers"* (v. 19). We'll cover this one in the next chapter.

10. *"She opens her arms to the poor and extends her hands to the needy"* (v. 20). Not only is this woman charitable and thoughtful of those less fortunate, she has enough to share with others. As positive wives let's open our eyes to the needs around us. And let's be responsible with our finances. Then when God shows us a need, we'll be able to extend a hand to help.

Be a Blessing!

Whatever financial mistakes we may have made in the past, let's determine to start today to be a blessing to our husbands and families by being responsible with the resources God has given us. It doesn't matter how much or how little we have. The issue is contentment. The call is to responsibility. Let's choose today to be content in our hearts and live responsibly with our hands. May it be said of us, as the writer of Proverbs says of the noble wife, "Many women do noble things, but you surpass them all" (Proverbs 31:29).

POWER POINT

⚙ **Read:** Proverbs speaks a great deal about the handling of money. The following verses offer a brief financial journey through this book of wisdom: Proverbs 3:27–28; 6:1, 6–8; 11:15; 20:4; 21:5, 20, 25–26; 22:1–4, 7, 26–27; 23:4–5; 24:3–6, 30–34; 28:19–20, 22. What sound financial principles do you find in these verses? What principles are repeated several times?

♡ **Pray:** Glorious Lord and awesome God, you are the great Provider. You take care of all my needs! Thank you that I can look to you for help and direction in my finances. Help me to be responsible in my spending and saving. Allow me to distinguish the difference between wants and needs. Open my eyes to the needs of others, and help me to be responsible with my money so that I have something to give to those in need. Oh, Lord, most importantly, help me to be content no matter what my circumstances are. Thank you for your wisdom, and help me to follow it day by day. In Jesus' name I pray, amen.

💡 **Remember:** "Not that I speak from want; for I have learned to be content in whatever circumstances I am" (Philippians 4:11 NASB).

☺ **Do:** Plan a time to sit down with your husband and go over financial matters. Decide together what spending, saving, and budgeting plans are best for your family. Identify ways each of you can adjust or change to meet the common goal of financial responsibility. Remember to honor your husband during this meeting. Be loving and respectful, not demanding or emotional.

Domestic Diva
Helpful Hints on Managing the Home Front

When friends enter a home they sense its personality and character, the family's style of living—these elements make a house come alive with a sense of identity, a sense of energy, enthusiasm, and warmth, declaring, this is who we are; this is how we live.

—Ralph Lauren

Today's To-Do List

1. Drive daughter to 6:00 A.M. cross-country practice at school, pick up her friend on the way.

2. Have a quiet time of prayer and Bible reading.

3. Prepare lunch for other daughter; taker her to school at 7:40 A.M.

4. Help Curt get out the door to the office with a fresh cup of coffee in hand.

5. Clean up kitchen, make bed, straighten house.

6. Answer e-mails.

7. Put load in washer.

8. Feed and brush dogs.

9. Return phone calls.

10. Deal with school-board issue.

11. Run by grocery store for forgotten items from yesterday's grocery-store visit.

12. Meet friend for lunch.

13. Stop by the bank.

14. Get an oil change for the car.

15. Write several more sections of chapter on household responsibility chapter for *Positive Wife* book.

16. Make phone calls to set appointments.

17. Write thank-you notes.

18. Pick up kids from school.

19. Help them with homework.

20. Prepare, eat, and clean up after dinner.

21. Fold clothes; put them away.

22. Take one daughter to kick boxing, the other to golf lesson.

23. Take a walk with Curt.

24. Read.

25. Go to bed.

Phew!

How does your to-do list look today? I have a feeling yours may be similar to mine. Most wives juggle a tremendous number of responsibilities at home, at work, and in the community. With schedules like ours, I doubt that many of us would dub ourselves the Martha Stewarts of the new millennium. Perhaps some wives are true domestic wonders and run smooth-sailing ships; but I think most of us struggle to keep our sea legs on deck as the waves of responsibility roll in, one after another, rocking our boats and threatening to sink us.

Here's a true confession: I'm not the perfect Proverbs 31 woman. Mrs. Proverbs 31 is the queen of her home, a gifted manager running the affairs of her household in a perfectly responsible way. When I read about her impeccable household and glowing life, I feel like a home-economics dropout in comparison. I'm disorganized. I've got clutter. And I certainly don't make my own linens, much less buy fields and plant vineyards in my spare time.

Perhaps you feel inadequate when you look at her life too. Don't despair. Whether we're perfectly organized, hopelessly messy, or some-where in between, I daresay each of us could use a little help in some area of our households. Take it from me, a domestic default: There is hope for us all.

It's hard to imagine any woman doing everything that Mrs. Proverbs 31 does. One Bible commentary suggests that this superlady might be a composite sketch of all the ideal qualities of a noble wife. The commentary goes on to warn, "Do not see her as a model to imi-tate in every detail; your days are not long enough to do everything she does."[1] In other words, we shouldn't expect to follow in her every foot-step; rather, we should see her as a model from whom we can learn and glean ideas on being positive wives.

We don't need to cringe in comparison. Instead, we can look at this woman in the same way a young girl looks at Miss America on TV. "Wow, I want to be just like her." The fact is, everyone—even Miss America and Mrs. Proverbs 31—has flaws and weaknesses. In this snapshot of the noble wife, we only see her glory. We can be inspired by her and learn from her; but we can also breathe a sigh of relief, because we know that a real woman also has a downside, complete with short-comings and inadequacies. Our goal isn't perfection. It's to be diligent and faithful with the gifts God has given us.

I have to admit, I wish her weaknesses were spelled out for us along with her strengths so that we could relate to her a little more easily. But then again, maybe her description in Proverbs 31 serves as a reminder that we should build on our strengths and not focus on our weaknesses. We can be gifts to our families—just as Mrs. Proverbs 31 was to hers—not by imitating her every move, but by demonstrating a similar sense of responsibility and diligence in our homes.

Household Agreements

Running a household is no piece of cake. When I think about the tasks that generally fall on a woman's shoulders, I sometimes want to scream, "Time out!" Why am I the one who is in charge of the laundry, the bills, the dinner, the housecleaning, the grocery shopping, and the kids' activities? Of course, your responsibilities may not be exactly the same as mine. Every couple's situation is different, which means the division of household responsibilities may be different. We each come into marriage with our own preconceived ideas about the duties of a husband and a wife. We also have different levels of responsibility outside the home.

There is no right or wrong way to figure out who does what. The important thing is for you and your husband to have a mutual understanding of one another's roles as you work through the responsibilities of your household together. At a time when you are both relaxed and comfortable, prayerfully discuss what a healthy balance of responsibilities would be in your home. Decide what each of you can do to support your marriage and the proper running of your household. Work together to divide the load as best you can.

Both of you will have to compromise. Even so, the way the tasks break down between the two of you may not seem completely fair. As a positive wife, be willing to take on more than your fair share. Here's why: No spouse sees the entire weight of the workload that the other spouse carries during the day. If you're going to err, err on the side of giving, not getting. Be faithful to keep up with your responsibilities and do your part to make the household run smoothly without focusing on what your husband is or is not doing.

If your husband is the sole breadwinner in the family, you can take on the major part of managing the home front. He can be more effective in his job if he is supported by a well-run home. Part of your role is understanding the struggles your husband may face in a typical day and recognizing that he may be coming home tired and weary. Perhaps he had to deal with a challenging situation or a difficult person at work; maybe he had to drive through an hour of bumper-to-bumper traffic. When he walks in the door, the last thing he needs is to be hit with a list of chores or a litany of complaints. (You can tell him your gripes and concerns later. Maybe they won't seem so important to you by then.) Instead, greet him with a smile and a hug and help him to feel glad to be there.

If both of you are employed, you will have to work harder to find a healthy balance between you. Consider each other's time and workload expended outside the home. Look for solutions to make your life together less stressful. If possible, pay someone else to do a chore, so that your time and energy can go into activities that you need to do yourself.

For years I cleaned my own house; but when I reached the point of writing almost full time, I started paying a maid to do what she does best, so I can do what I do best. I also used to cook dinner every night of the week. I felt guilty if I didn't. But on those afternoons when I was in the car from 3:30 to 7:00 P.M., shuttling the kids to and from all their activities, I couldn't get dinner on the table until just before 8:00. I finally realized that my responsibility is to provide a dinner for my family, whether I cook it or not. Sometimes takeout from a local restaurant works just as well as home cooking (and tastes a whole lot better). Consider the cost; look for coupons; but pay for help when you can.

The house of every one is to him his castle and fortress. —Sir Edward Coke

When dividing domestic tasks, take into account the unique gifts, abilities, and talents each of you possesses. In our family Curt is the decorator, both inside the house and out in the garden. He is gifted at it, and he loves it. I don't; so gardening, lawn maintenance, and decorating the house fall into his domain. On the other hand, I write the bills, do laundry, and handle household maintenance.

After the two of you have determined what is right, reasonable, and fair for both of you to do around the house, set in your mind that you will always do more than your fair share. Don't grumble, nag, or complain (how unbecoming of a positive wife!). Instead, move forward prayerfully and cheerfully in God's strength. The blessing of a well-run home will be your reward.

Don't Be a Nag!

I should probably say a few more words about nagging, because it's such an easy thing for wives to fall into. Let's face it. Our husbands don't always keep up their end of the bargain, and nagging seems to come naturally to us in those moments. Maybe your husband is sitting on the couch watching TV, even though the kids need their bath (the job he agreed to do). Maybe he hasn't taken out the garbage yet, and tomorrow is trash day. You mention it once: "Honey, it's almost time for the kids to go to bed, and they really need a bath first." Or, "Sweetheart, did you remember that trash day is tomorrow?" But he hasn't moved an inch.

You're not going to nag, are you? Let's identify nagging so you know what it looks like. How else can you guard against it? Typically nagging shows up in one or a combination of the following, depending on the circumstances:

1. Repeating a command or demand more than once

2. Using a disrespectful or whiny tone

3. Huffing off when he doesn't do what you want him to do

4. Grumbling and complaining aloud or under your breath

5. Standing over him with your arms crossed, tapping your big toe on the floor, or wagging your pointer finger in his face

6. Giving the silent treatment

If you can't nag, what *can* you do? Here are a few simple rules for getting your husband to do his part around the house.

Rule #1: Clearly communicate the details of what you expect.

Most nagging can be eliminated from the onset through good communication and realistic expectations. Often, nagging is the result of trying to get our husbands to do things they never agreed to do in the first place.

Be reasonable and realistic in your expectations of what "must be done" by your spouse. And recognize when you need to back off. Some things can wait, but for some unknown reason we want them done *now*. If the need is not immediate, relax a little and determine a reasonable time frame for finishing the task. The more you bring your husband in on the thinking process, the less imploring you will need to do.

Rule #2: Speak in a kind, soothing, and respectful voice.

A rude tone of voice can cause your husband to dig in his heels all the more. You can be firm, yet loving. Serious, yet kind. Use your voice and tone diplomatically to get the best results.

Rule #3: Explain the consequences.

Say, "If you don't stop by the store on your way home from work, we won't have any milk for your cereal in the morning." Or, "If you don't put out the trash tonight, our backyard will smell like rotten eggs until the next trash day." It doesn't hurt to set a humorous tone! For example: "If the garage isn't cleaned out by winter, you're not going to have a place to put the car, and you're going to get very cold scraping the ice off your windshield every morning."

Rule #4: Be open for a good trade.

Instead of nagging, offer to trade one of your jobs for his. "Hey, honey, I'll make a deal with you. If you can't give the kids their bath now, I'll take care of it tonight, and you can take care of writing the bills for me tomorrow night." Guys love bargaining power!

Rule #5: If applicable, offer to pay someone else to do it.

Depending on what needs to be done, suggest paying someone else to do the task. This will accomplish one of two things: It will either shift him into high gear because he is a miser and doesn't want to pay money out of his pocket; or it will make him happy because the job is off his shoulders and you are off his back. Either way, the job gets done.

Getting Organized

On my bookshelf I probably have ten books telling me how to schedule my days, organize my household, and get a handle on house-keeping. Each book is packed full of wonderful, creative ways to use my time wisely and keep my home in tip-top shape. Unfortunately, most of the books could have the same subtitle: *Thousands of Great Ideas That Nobody Actually Puts into Practice.*

In this chapter, I don't want to overwhelm you with a myriad of ideas. I just want to share a few solid, practical tips that can make a lasting difference in our homes and in our lives.

Organizing Stuff

Even a naturally messy person like me can learn to maintain a neat and tidy environment. How? By following these three simple steps.

1. Remember the adage "A place for everything, and everything in its place."

When you know where a certain item belongs, it's easier to return it to its place. Think of yourself as a placement expert, getting all the lost articles in your house to their proper homes. You can even have a location for all the items that you want to deal with later—just make sure you also choose a time each week to eliminate the junk pile. Which leads me to my next point:

2. Designate a time to kill piles and annihilate clutter.

Set a specific time each week for dealing with outstanding piles and help yourself by being clutter conscious throughout the week. Stuff can pile up so quickly! Mail is one of the biggies. When the mail arrives, stand by a trash can and go through it. Throw away junk mail and things you know you will never read. Then place bills in their proper place and read the letters you need to see right away.

Make it a nightly routine to clear the kitchen table and countertops of excess stuff and put utensils and appliances in order. You'll go to bed feeling you've accomplished something, and you'll wake up to a clean kitchen. It's the best way to start the day!

3. Create a personal game plan for cleaning the house.

You may choose to clean half the house one day and the other half another day. Or maybe you'd rather clean the bathrooms one day, the bedrooms on a second day, and the kitchen and living room on a third. Laundry can also be done by routine. I usually do my husband's laundry on Monday, mine on Tuesday, and my daughters' on Wednesday and Thursday.

(For more help getting a handle on household cleaning, I recommend two excellent Internet sources: the FlyLady Web site at www.flylady.net and Sidetracked Home Executives at www.shesorganized.com.)

Organizing Time

An important aspect of managing the home front is organization. Actually we don't literally organize our time; we organize *ourselves* within the twenty-four hours that God has given us each day. If you're like me, you probably find yourself wishing you had more hours in the day. What we really need to wish is that we would make wiser decisions about what to do with the time we have. We'll get a lot more done by making better choices than by hoping that God miraculously creates a twenty-seven-hour day.

Here are a few basic principles of sound time management.

1. Get up early.

One thing we must admire about Mrs. Proverbs 31 is that she uses her time to the fullest. We read in Proverbs 31:15 that "she gets up while it is still dark" to provide food for her family. In other words, she doesn't sleep in. She jumps into her day with vigor. We are also told in Mark 1:35 that "very early in the morning, while it was still dark, Jesus got up, left the house and went off to a solitary place, where he prayed." Put those two verses together, and you have a tremendous way for positive wives to start their day—up early, praying, and providing!

Let's not get legalistic. If you've been up through the night with a nursing baby or sick child, or you're struggling with illness yourself, then by all means, catch up on your sleep! We all need to get adequate rest. Otherwise, keep in mind the old adage by Ben Franklin: "Early to bed, early to rise, makes a man [or woman] healthy, wealthy, and wise."

2. Make the best use of your calendar.

I carry my calendar/planner with me wherever I go. In addition to daily and monthly calendar sections, it has an address book where I

She watches over the affairs of her household and does not eat the bread of idleness. —Proverbs 31:27

keep important numbers and information. Whenever I need to schedule a meeting or a date, I put it on my monthly calendar. I plan my day and write down my phone messages on my daily calendar. On Sunday afternoon (a day of reflection and renewal for me) I look over my calendar for the coming week, pray for upcoming events, and jot down any activities that involve my husband and children on the family calendar I keep in the kitchen.

3. Choose wisely what you will do.

Our society offers so many great opportunities, we could be busy with activities almost every hour of the day and night if we wanted to. How do you decide what to do—and what not to do? I like what Paul said to the Thessalonians: "Examine everything carefully; hold fast to that which is good" (1 Thessalonians 5:21 NASB). Give careful consideration to what you put on your calendar. And remember to factor in your kids' activities. They become your activities, too, as you spend your time driving to and from piano lessons, ballet, soccer, and Little League. So before you commit yourself to obligations galore, ask yourself:

- Is this what God would have me do with my time?
- Why do I want to do it?
- Is my husband supportive, or does he have valid objections?
- Does it fit with my life purpose and goals?
- Does it develop and utilize my talents?

Learn to say no! Ecclesiastes 3:1 reminds us, "There is a time for everything, and a season for every activity under heaven." There is a time for everything, and that time may not be today. It may not be this year. Ask God to help you choose the things he wants you to be doing right now.

4. Plan your day the night before.

Before you nod off to Never Never Land, take a look at your calendar and see what you have scheduled for the next day. Write down the errands you need to run and the places you need to go and make a general plan. As you sink into bed, pray for the next day while it's fresh on your mind.

5. Review your week on Sunday.

Sunday is a good day to look over the coming week, pray it through, and plot it out. Put time on your schedule for friends, responsibilities, and personal interests.

6. Maintain a healthy balance.

It's a good idea to take a step back now and then and check the balance of your life. Are you maintaining strong friendships with other women? Are you growing spiritually? Intellectually? Are you taking care of yourself physically? Have you let one or more areas of your life slide and get out of balance? I use January 1 of each new year for setting goals and doing this kind of maintenance check.

Response Ability

As we close out this chapter, I want to turn the focus away from ourselves for just a moment. It's easy to become so totally caught up in our own households, our own schedules, and our own lives that we forget about the needs of others. Our responsibility is not only to our homes and our jobs. When we order our households and schedule our time, we must do so with an eye to serving in our churches and communities too. God has given us wonderful gifts and talents that are not meant to be kept within the four walls of the home front.

I think of Clara McBride Hale, a devoted and loving mother who raised her own children—along with over thirty other kids. It was her unconditional love for children that led her to open Hale House in Harlem, New York, in the early 1970s, as a center to help babies born to mothers addicted to drugs. Even today, the legacy of this remarkable woman lives on in Dr. Lorraine Hale, Clara's daughter, who serves as the administrator of Hale House. The center still provides love, nurture, and medical attention to precious and helpless babies.

In 1985 President Ronald Reagan named "Mother" Clara McBride Hale an "American hero"—even though she claimed she was simply "a person who loves children."[2] God used her love, determination, and gifting not only to bless her own family but also to make a lasting impact in her community. She saw a need outside her own four walls and responded with her abilities. What needs do you see? What abilities has God given you? Now pray, "God, how do you want me to respond?"

The Best Employer

Remember, whether you are working inside or outside the home, in your family or in your community, as a Christian you have an awesome Employer. You're not simply working for the boss at the office, the manager in the field, the editor, the community center director, or your husband and kids; you are working for the Lord. Colossians 3:23–24 reminds us, "Work hard and cheerfully at whatever you do, as though you were working for the Lord rather than for people. Remember that the Lord will give you an inheritance as your reward, and the Master you are serving is Christ" (NLT).

Personally, when I realize I'm working for God, not just people, I get a little extra spring in my step and gas in my tank. It's not often that you and I get a pat on the back or a word of praise for all that we do. But as positive wives, we can fulfill our many responsibilities in and out of our homes with continuous joy, because we know that we answer ultimately to God. He's our great Employer; and as we're faithful, one day we'll hear him say, "Well done."

POWER POINT

⚙ **Read:** Titus 2:3–5 and Proverbs 31:19–29. What are some of the responsibilities presented in these verses? If you were to describe the women in these passages, what positive words would you use? Could someone use these same words to describe you?

♡ **Pray:** O Lord, you are all I need! Thank you for the abilities and talents you have given me. Help me to use these gifts in my home and my community. Make me a blessing to all those around me, especially my husband. Show the two of us how to work well together as a couple. Please help me to understand a little more of the burden he bears in the work he does. Help me to organize my home and my time to the best of my abilities, and help me to maintain a healthy balance in my life. Thank you for always being with me. You are the best Employer! I love you. In Jesus' name, amen.

💡 **Remember:** "Whatever you do, work at it with all your heart, as working for the Lord, not for men" (Colossians 3:23).

☺ **Do:** Take a look at your life from the perspective of how you are using your time right now. Make a list of the activities in which you are currently involved, along with the responsibilities you have at home and in your community. Are there any areas that need to change? Should you be doing more? Or are you doing too much and need to slow down? Talk it over with your husband; he may have a unique perspective and some good ideas about how to best use your time. Plan to do this kind of deliberate examination of your responsibilities at least once a year.

Power Principle #7

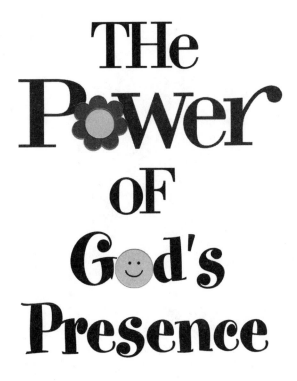

THe P⚘wer of G☺d's Presence

Delight yourself in the LORD; and He will give you the desires of your heart. Commit your way to the LORD, trust also in Him, and He will do it.

—Psalm 37:4–5 NASB

Love has its source in God, for love is the very essence of His being.

—Kay Arthur

16

Intimate Fellowship
The Secret to Becoming a Holy and Happy Wife

*No time is so well spent in every day as that
which we spend upon our knees.*

—J. C. Ryle

William Law once said, "He who has learned to pray has learned the greatest secret of a holy and happy life."[1] I suppose we could personalize that statement to fit positive wives, for most certainly the wife who has learned to pray has learned the secret to a holy and happy life. There is nothing more vital to a positive marriage than a wife's commitment to prayer. Don't think because this chapter comes near the end of the book that prayer is a lesser principle than the others in our quest to be positive wives. Every principle we've discussed up to this point depends greatly on this particular one.

Oh, how foolish we are when we try to hold our marriages together without the presence of God! I don't know your situation. Perhaps you are married to a wonderful, godly man. Or maybe you are married to a Christian man who is not walking closely with God. It could be that your husband is not a Christian at all. Whatever the case, you are responsible for your own relationship and fellowship with God, not your husband's. If this were a marriage book for couples, I would tell you both about the beauty and blessing of growing in prayer together. But this is a book to you as a wife; and whether you have the opportunity to pray with your spouse or not, you always have the ability to fellowship with God on your own.

Prayer is not simply coming to God with a list of requests. Rather, it is a precious time of fellowship with our heavenly Father, the Creator of the universe and the Lover of our souls. Why would we neglect so great an opportunity and so intimate a communion? Yet we do. For whatever reason—our busy schedules, our lack of faith, our misplaced priorities— many of us don't spend the time with God that we know we should. As a result, we miss out on a deeper relationship with the only One who can provide a grounding for our souls and an anchor for our lives.

Let's take the next few pages to look at what prayer can mean to us as positive wives.

Fellowship with the Father

In the deepest of relationships, there exists a continual flow of communication and fellowship. In a soul-mate relationship, for example, conversation is frequent and rarely one sided. I think of the communication between a married couple as the conduit for deeper understanding and oneness. In my own marriage, I enjoy the times Curt and I can communicate during the day, and I especially look forward to his phone calls when he is out of town. Imagine how difficult it would be for Curt and me to know one another intimately if we never talked to each other!

Prayer is intimate communication with God. It's how we grow deeper in our faith, our love, and our walk with him. We need to set aside time for prayer—time for communing with God, reading his Word, and casting our cares at his feet. The result of this intimate fellowship with God is the development of a beautiful relationship. Oh, the bond that grows from this intentional time of prayer!

What part does prayer play in your life right now? For some women, prayer is segregated to Sundays at church and maybe a weekly group Bible study. For others, it consists of those few sentences of grace spoken at the dinner table just before digging in. Oh sure, many Christians talk about prayer. But much too often the old, familiar "I'll be praying for you" could be better translated "I'm sure hopeful for you," because the last thing we plan to do is actually pray about the situation. Can you relate?

Making the decision to meet with God each day takes discipline and devotion. It's helpful to have a specific time and place set aside for these times of fellowship with the Father.

During my sophomore year in college, I got together with a particular "guy friend" once a week for lunch. We had a standing date every Friday at a little sandwich shop just off campus. We met there to visit and encourage one another. We had our place and time, and we kept our appointment like clockwork throughout the year.

Designating a time and place to meet with God helps create a routine. Not that our prayer lives should become old and routine! No, prayer can grow continually and become more vibrant and abundant each day. But it must begin with the discipline and commitment to "be there."

Meeting early in the morning—as Jesus did, according to Mark 1:35—involves an even greater commitment. Like Jesus, David also met with God in the early hours of the day. This man after God's own heart said, "In the morning, O LORD, you hear my voice; in the morning I lay my requests before you and wait in expectation" (Psalm 5:3). Why morning? It's the perfect time to set the new day before the Lord. Before we begin to worry, fret, and proceed in our own power and strength, we can give our cares and worries to our heavenly Father and leave them there. Robert Murray M'Cheyne put it this way: "Let us see God before man every day."[2]

By starting our day in fellowship with the Lord, we are more apt to recognize and enjoy his presence all day long. What a joy it is to walk with God throughout the challenges of the day; yet how sorrowful (and scary) our day can be if we choose to walk without him! My friend Janet Holm McHenry, author of *Prayer Walk* (WaterBrook Press), discovered the joy and impact of morning prayer as she went on walks in the early hours of the day. Her walks became her time of fellowship with the Father and literally revolutionized her life. Janet found that as she grew in her prayer life in the mornings, she became more aware of ways to pray for others throughout the day.

As we do the laundry, clean the house, and run errands, you and I can walk and talk with God all day long. At work, at school, at soccer games, we can continue to commune with him. Waiting in line behind an angry person at the bank, driving by the scene of an accident, or noticing a sad face in the mall becomes an opportunity to pray. As positive wives we can start the day in prayer and then practice God's presence all day long, recognizing that his Spirit dwells within us. We are not walking alone!

In the Secret Place

William Wilberforce said, "Of all things, guard against neglecting God in the secret place of prayer."[3] But what do we say to God in that secret place? How do we communicate with the Creator of the universe? The very thought is overwhelming! Perhaps that's how one of the disciples felt when he said to Jesus, "Lord, teach us to pray." In response, Jesus gave the sample prayer found in Luke 11:2–4. You'll notice that it's similar to the sample prayer he gave in his Sermon on the Mount. Although this is a prayer we repeat often in church, it was not given to us as a passage to recite, but as an example from which to learn. Here it is in the New Living Translation of the Bible:

Father, may your name be honored.
May your Kingdom come soon.
Give us our food day by day.
And forgive us our sins—
Just as we forgive those who have sinned against us.
And don't let us yield to temptation.

We can glean many important truths from Jesus' sample prayer. Let's take a moment to reflect on each line.

"Father, may your name be honored." As we enter God's presence, we come before the high King of heaven. Imagine having an audience with the king of a foreign nation, and instead of greeting him with honor and praise, we walk right in and begin making requests or chatting away. If we would not treat a human dignitary with such disrespect, why would we come before our great and holy heavenly King in such a manner? In humble recognition of our lowly estate and his high position, we must come into God's presence with the respect and honor that is due him. We esteem him, not because he is an arrogant king who demands it, but because we recognize that he alone is worthy of all honor, glory, and praise.

"May your Kingdom come soon." This statement is a recognition that we are not living simply for this world. It's a realization that we are looking forward to another day, a better day. When we turn our eyes heavenward, we get an eternal focus that shakes everything here on earth down to its proper level of importance. James warns, "When you ask, you do not receive, because you ask with wrong motives, that you

You are my portion, O LORD; I have promised to obey your words. —Psalm 119:57

☺

237

may spend what you get on your pleasures" (James 4:3). Having a heavenly focus makes us more apt to pray according to God's eternal will rather than on the basis of our own immediate wants or needs.

In the corresponding prayer in the Sermon on the Mount, Jesus adds this line: "May your will be done here on earth, just as it is in heaven" (Matthew 6:10 NLT). Theologian John Stott says of this verse, "Prayer is not a convenient device for imposing our will upon God, or for bending his will to ours, but the prescribed way of subordinating our will to his. It is by prayer that we seek God's will, embrace it and align ourselves with it. Every true prayer is a variation on the theme, 'Your will be done.' Our Master taught us to say this in the pattern prayer he gave us, and added the supreme example of it in Gethsemane."[4]

"Give us our food day by day." As I read this line, I am reminded of the Israelites as they wandered in the wilderness for forty years. God provided the food they needed each day, no more and no less. They were dependent on his provision daily. In this sample prayer, we're taught to request the daily necessities of life, realizing that God is the provider. We're not in charge of meeting our needs; God is. This request reminds us of our dependence on him.

"Forgive us our sins..." This is something only God can do—and oh, how we need it!

"...just as we forgive those who have sinned against us." Our forgiveness of others is a biggie with God. Why? Because when we don't forgive others, we show that we've forgotten our humble estate. We've put out of our minds our own need for forgiveness. We've forgotten that we've been forgiven of all our sins through the mercy of God. Since God has forgiven us, we must in turn forgive those who have wronged us.

As we come before the Lord daily, we must bring our burden of sin and lay it before him, knowing that in Christ we are forgiven and cleansed. Then we must ask God to show us any bitterness, anger, or unforgiveness we are holding against others, and we must release it. As we free other people by forgiving them, we free ourselves to live and love.

Forgiveness must begin with our spouses, as we learned in chapter 4. When we release the anger and unforgiveness we feel toward our husbands, we—and they—can move forward. So can our marriages. If we hold on to resentment, however, it only festers and grows into a deeper bitterness and separation. We become ugly with hatred. Truly, unforgiveness is one of the most unlovely traits a wife can have!

As positive wives we need to live in the much more lovely state of forgiveness and prayer. God will heal our marriages and our relationships as we faithfully forgive those who have wronged us. Of course, forgiveness is not always easy. We need to seek God's help. But rest assured that if he tells us to forgive, he will provide the strength and the ability to accomplish it.

"And don't let us yield to temptation." When was the last time you prayed that God would help you steer clear of sin and give you victory in the midst of temptation? I've got to admit, I rarely pray that way. I'm usually too busy praying for my long list of needs and wants. How about you?

If we're going to be successful in our marriages and effective in all the things God has called us to do, then we need to ask for his help in not succumbing to the temptations around us. What tempts you? Often I think of the big areas of sin and figure I'm doing quite well. *I'm not stealing, committing adultery, or killing anyone,* I think, *so I must be doing pretty good.*

Hmmmm. Then gossip and overindulgence and unforgiveness and discontentment and grumbling come to mind, and I begin to realize that I am faced with heavy temptations every day. I not only need

God's help to see the temptations; I need his strength to keep from yielding to them. Can you relate? Perhaps you want to pray with me: *Lord, open our eyes to the temptations around us. Help us to recognize sin and turn from it!*

Praying for Our Husbands

In our times of prayer, one of the high honors and privileges we have is to pray for our spouses. Yet so often it seems that we only come to God in distress: "Lord, fix this awful trait in my husband!" What greater joy would we experience if we would learn to pray not in distress, but in love and blessing?

We actually grow deeper in our love for our husbands as we faithfully pray for their physical, emotional, and spiritual needs. A positive wife is a praying wife! Let's look at several important ways we can lift up our husbands in prayer.

Be thankful for him.

The apostle Paul closes his letter to the Thessalonians with an uplifting word of encouragement: "Be joyful always; pray continually; give thanks in all circumstances, for this is God's will for you in Christ Jesus" (1 Thessalonians 5:16–18). What good words for us as positive, praying wives! I truly believe that as we pray continually and give thanks in all things, we will be joyful always. As we get our minds off what is wrong with our husbands and begin thanking God for them, our hearts will begin to change toward them in positive ways.

How should you begin? Start by thanking God for the good traits you see in your husband. Thank God for bringing this man into your life. Thank God for the things you saw in him that brought you together in the first place. You may want to write these positive traits in

I have sought your face with all my heart; be gracious to me according to your promise. —Psalm 119:58

a prayer journal and keep adding to the list as you think of additional ones. The more we thank God for our spouses' wonderful traits, the more we'll see.

Now here's the more difficult task: Paul says we should give thanks in *all* circumstances, not just the good ones. Are you ready to thank the Lord for the difficult traits in your spouse? Can you thank God for his weaknesses? I don't want to encourage you to dwell on your husband's bad points or enumerate them; I simply want you to thank God for those areas. Thank God for how he can use those traits in your husband to do a greater work in your life. Just as "iron sharpens iron" (Proverbs 27:17), sometimes the things in another person that rub us the wrong way are the very things that can polish our character.

Pray for his needs.

God frequently encourages us in Scripture to bring our needs and cares before him. In Matthew 7:7, Jesus himself implores us to ask of God through prayer. We don't have to hold back when it comes to asking God to provide for our husbands!

What should we ask for? I think again of Jesus' sample prayer. In those simple verses I'm reminded of at least seven specific things that we can pray for our husbands:

1. Pray that he honors God's name—that he reveres the Lord and walks in a manner worthy of his calling (Ephesians 4:1; Colossians 1:9–10). If he is not a Christian, pray that he comes to know Jesus as his Savior (Romans 10:13).

2. Pray that he has an eternal perspective in life; that he looks forward to God's kingdom; that his heart and mind are focused on things above (Colossians 3:1–2). Pray that he is not conformed

to this world, but transformed by the renewing of his mind (Romans 12:2).

3. Pray that he sees God as the provider of all his needs (Proverbs 30:8; Philippians 4:19) and that he continues to seek God's direction each day (Proverbs 3:5–6).

4. Pray that as he enjoys God's forgiveness, he will in turn walk in forgiveness toward others (Ephesians 4:32).

5. Pray that he would not yield to temptation and that God would deliver him from evil (Matthew 6:13; James 4:7). Pray also that he would stand firm against the schemes of the devil, putting on the full armor of God (Ephesians 6:10–18).

6. Pray that the Holy Spirit would be at work in his life and that the fruit of the Spirit would be evident in his actions (Galatians 5:22–23).

7. Pray that he would love the Lord with all his heart, mind, soul, and strength and that he would demonstrate Christ's love to others (Matthew 22:37–38; 1 John 4:7–21).

The list could go on, but this is a starting point at least. Since we've identified seven areas of prayer, you might want to consider praying for one area each day of the week (number one on Sunday, number two on Monday, and so on). You can pray confidently for each of these things on your husband's behalf. You know you are asking according to God's will, because each request is based upon his Word.

Don't give up!

Perhaps you're thinking, *But you don't know my husband. If there ever was a case too hard to crack, it's him.* You're right; I don't know your husband. Perhaps you've already been praying for him for some time. But let me encourage you: Don't lose heart. No matter how hopeless it seems, never give up. Continue in faithful prayer and put your hope and trust in God. Jesus encouraged his followers to persist in prayer by giving this illustration in Luke 18:1–5:

> Then Jesus told his disciples a parable to show them that they should always pray and not give up. He said: "In a certain town there was a judge who neither feared God nor cared about men. And there was a widow in that town who kept coming to him with the plea, 'Grant me justice against my adversary.'
>
> "For some time he refused. But finally he said to himself, 'Even though I don't fear God or care about men, yet because this widow keeps bothering me, I will see that she gets justice, so that she won't eventually wear me out with her coming!'"

In these words Jesus was telling us not to lose heart in prayer. Persist, even if the results you seek don't seem to be forthcoming. Thankfully, just as a good and loving father doesn't give his children everything they want right when they want it, so our heavenly Father works on his timetable, not ours. I am so awed by the complexity of God! He doesn't work in the simplistic ways we would choose. He isn't into the quick-fix programs we would prefer. As Isaiah 55:8–9 affirms, his ways are different than our ways, and his thoughts are much higher than our thoughts.

It may be years before you see the answer to your prayers. Trust God; trust that his plan is much bigger than what you can see. He loves your husband much more than you do. It's his desire that no person should perish and that all believers should be conformed to the image of his Son, Jesus. He alone knows what it will take to make these things happen in your husband's life. Your part, and mine, is to do what Paul tells us in Colossians 4:2: "Devote yourselves to prayer, being watchful and thankful."

The Beauty Shop of Prayer

Earlier we said that unforgiveness is a very unlovely quality in a wife. Another unlovely quality is prayerlessness. Dr. Joseph Parker says, "You can tell whether a man has been keeping up his life of prayer. His witness is in his face. That face grows in vulgarity which does not commune with God day by day. It loses beauty. 'The show of their countenance doth witness against them.' There is an invisible sculptor that chisels the face into the upper attitude of the soul."[5]

The best beauty tip I can give you is this: Spend time daily in the beauty shop of prayer. That's where your beauty is developed beyond the surface level, down to the very depths of your heart and soul. Meeting with God each day is better than any beauty treatment money can buy. A positive wife who meets continually with God, who relishes his love and casts her cares and worries on him, will have a demeanor of confidence and brightness that her husband and everyone else around her will see. Deborah put it this way in her song of victory in Judges 5:31: "May those who love the Lord shine as the sun" (TLB).

The key to a holy, happy, and beautiful life is a lifestyle of prayer and intimate fellowship with God. As positive wives let's be praying wives. That way we'll be sure to shine.

POWER POINT

⚙ **Read:** Matthew 6:25–34. What do you learn about God in this passage? What place should worry have in your life? Now read Matthew 7:7–12. What three verbs are given to us in the way of instruction in prayer? Are you practicing these in your life?

♥ **Pray:** O wonderful Father, Savior, and Friend, how perfect you are! Thank you that through Jesus' death on the cross for my sins, I have the opportunity to come before your throne and meet with you. Thank you for hearing my prayers and asking me to come to you with my requests. Help me to be faithful in setting aside time to be with you. I want to walk closely with you each day. You are my soul mate! My desire is for you, and my longing is for intimate fellowship with you. Keep my heart on things above, and do not let me stray from your principles. I love you! In Jesus' name I pray, amen.

♀ **Remember:** "Be joyful always; pray continually; give thanks in all circumstances, for this is God's will for you in Christ Jesus" (1 Thessalonians 5:16–18).

☺ **Do:** Set aside a time and choose a place to meet with God each day. Then start meeting. This takes discipline, so be diligent. In your quiet moments with the Lord, delight in him! That's the key to a peaceful, joyful, and holy life.

17

God's Love Letters
Enjoying the Treasures of His Word

Too many married people expect their partner to give that which only God can give, namely, an eternal ecstasy.

—Fulton Sheen

Imagine visiting an old, run-down antique store nestled in the town square of a small English village. As you walk to the back of the store, you're intrigued by the sight of a large storage chest that is dusty and worn. The shopkeeper approaches you and says, "That's an old treasure chest from thirteenth-century England. Open it up." As you gingerly put your hand to the chest and slowly open the top, you see a brilliant and beautiful treasure inside. You run your hands through piles of gold coins. You gaze with wonder at jeweled crowns, ruby pendants, and pearl necklaces. You stand in amazement, awed by the sight of such great riches.

"Go ahead. Take a few jewels," the shopkeeper says. "That's fine with me. You keep them as my gift."

At first you think, *Yeah, right. What's the catch?* But then you realize the shopkeeper is serious. He wants you to take some treasure, no strings attached. He even invites you to come back for more. Finally you take a gold nugget and vow to return to the store quite often. As you walk away you think to yourself, *Why doesn't everyone go in there and gather some of the treasure that's free for the taking?*

Sound like a far-fetched story? It's not as odd as you may think. We have a treasure chest within our grasp every day. Some people pull it out on Sundays and remove a few gems. Others never peek inside. A few wise people open it up and glean from it on a daily basis. I'm speaking, of course, of the treasure chest of God's Word. Think of the riches that are available to us in Scripture! When we open its pages, we find pearls of great wisdom, gems of God's love, gold nuggets of faith, and crowns filled with bright jewels of hope.

Pennies from Heaven

During our engagement Curt was working in Houston, and I was working and planning our wedding in Dallas. The separation was difficult for us, but we made the best of it, straddling the distance with many phone calls and lots of letters. Every time I went to the mailbox and saw a letter from Curt, my heart would race until I could open the envelope, see his handwriting, and pour over his words of love. In the mix of mail were other envelopes, packages, and junk mail, but those pieces were meaningless next to Curt's letters. When it came to mail, what mattered to me was who sent it! A form letter from a political organization just didn't carry the same appeal as a handwritten message from my beloved fiancé.

The Bible is a love letter to each of us that comes from the heart of our loving heavenly Father. According to 2 Timothy 3:16, each word is God-breathed! The fact that it's from the almighty God and Creator of the universe makes it more compelling than any other letter we could ever open. I don't want to miss one word of it, do you?

In fact, the Bible is more than a love letter; it's the instruction manual for life, written by the very Maker of life. I must confess, I'm not one to read the instruction manual when I buy a new DVD player or coffee maker. Sadly, many people treat the manual for life the same way. Why do so many of us neglect to read the Bible? I think it comes down to one of two reasons.

1. People don't believe the Bible is actually God's Word.

But in 2 Peter 1:20–21 we read, "Above all, you must understand that no prophecy of Scripture came about by the prophet's own interpretation. For prophecy never had its origin in the will of man, but men spoke from God as they were carried along by the Holy Spirit." The Bible is not a hodgepodge collection by a bunch of men who threw together their ideas; rather, it's a perfect and complete volume inspired from beginning to end by the Holy Spirit of God, who did the writing through men.

Think about it. Over a period of fifteen hundred years, the Bible was penned by more than forty different people with a variety of backgrounds and experiences. Despite the variations in time and writers, this incredible work demonstrates a marvelous unity in all areas—historically, theologically, geographically, topically, and bio-graphically.[1] It's truly a miraculous compilation, designed and breathed into life by our God and Creator and put onto paper in the handwriting of mankind.

2. People think the Bible is filled with lists of "don't do this, don't do that," and they're turned off.

The truth is, the Bible is an incredibly positive, uplifting book. In his abundant love toward us, God uses Scripture to tell us how to travel successfully down the road of life. He warns us of those hindrances to the journey that we should steer clear of, and he tells us how to experience great joy along the way. In Psalm 119 we can read the psalmists' expressions of deep devotion and love toward the wonder of God's

Word. Here are just a few of the passages that extol the benefits and blessings of Scripture. These verses, taken from the New Living Translation, encourage us to embrace the Word of God with our whole being:

> I have hidden your word in my heart, that I might not sin against you. Blessed are you, O Lord; teach me your principles. I have recited aloud all the laws you have given us. I have rejoiced in your decrees as much as in riches. I will study your commandments and reflect on your ways. I will delight in your principles and not forget your word. (vv. 11–16)

> Teach me, O Lord, to follow every one of your principles. Give me understanding and I will obey your law; I will put it into practice with all my heart. Make me walk along the path of your commands, for that is where my happiness is found. (vv. 33–35)

> I reflect at night on who you are, O Lord, and I obey your law because of this. This is my happy way of life: obeying your commandments. Lord, you are mine! I promise to obey your words! With all my heart I want your blessings. Be merciful just as you promised. (vv. 55–58)

> Forever, O Lord, your word stands firm in heaven. Your faithfulness extends to every generation, as enduring as the earth you created. Your laws remain true today, for everything serves your plans. If your law hadn't sustained me with joy, I would have died in my misery. I will never forget your commandments, for you have used them to restore my joy and health. (vv. 89–93)

> Oh, how I love your law! I think about it all day long. Your commands make me wiser than my enemies, for your commands are my constant guide. (vv. 97–98)

How sweet are your words to my taste; they are sweeter than honey. (v. 103)

Your word is a lamp for my feet and a light for my path. (v. 105)

If we'll just take the time to examine it, we'll find that the Bible is a gloriously positive book filled with hope for the future and wisdom for the present, written by a loving God who wants the best for his beloved people. Like any truly loving father, he gives us instructions and rules as well as encouragement and love. If we'll drink in the nourishment of his Word on a regular basis, we're bound to flourish and grow in his loving care.

His Words for Marriage

As positive wives we must be women of wisdom. I'm not talking about the kind of "book knowledge" that comes with a high-school diploma or college degree. I'm talking about the godly wisdom that leads us to use discretion in our words and actions, especially in our marriages. I'm talking about the pearls of wisdom we can only find in the treasure chest of God.

The following scriptures can be applied to various aspects and areas in marriage. Isn't it wonderful to know that the God of love, our wonderful heavenly Father, desires the best for our marriages and encourages us through his Word to be positive wives? I want to encourage you not only to read the following verses with the intent of gaining wisdom but also to memorize the ones that particularly apply to your life. Oh, the beauty that is reflected in the life of a woman who adorns herself with the pearls of wisdom found in the Bible!

A Christlike Attitude

Your attitude should be the same as that of Christ Jesus: Who, being in very nature God, did not consider equality with God

I rejoice at Your word as one who finds great treasure. —Psalm 119:162 NKJV

251

something to be grasped, but made himself nothing, taking the very nature of a servant, being made in human likeness. (Philippians 2:5–7)

Be completely humble and gentle; be patient, bearing with one another in love. Make every effort to keep the unity of the Spirit through the bond of peace. (Ephesians 4:2–3)

Commitment

May the Lord direct your hearts into God's love and Christ's perseverance. (2 Thessalonians 3:5)

Until I come, devote yourself to the public reading of Scripture, to preaching and to teaching....Be diligent in these matters; give yourself wholly to them, so that everyone may see your progress. Watch your life and doctrine closely. Persevere in them, because if you do, you will save both yourself and your hearers. (1 Timothy 4:13, 15–16)

Love must be sincere. Hate what is evil; cling to what is good. Be devoted to one another in brotherly love. Honor one another above yourselves. Never be lacking in zeal, but keep your spiritual fervor, serving the Lord. Be joyful in hope, patient in affliction, faithful in prayer. (Romans 12:9–12)

Godly Love

Love is patient, love is kind. It does not envy, it does not boast, it is not proud. It is not rude, it is not self-seeking, it is not easily angered, it keeps no record of wrongs. Love does not delight in evil but rejoices with the truth. It always protects, always trusts, always hopes, always perseveres. (1 Corinthians 13:4–7)

God is love. Whoever lives in love lives in God, and God in him. In this way, love is made complete among us so that we will have confidence on the day of judgment, because in this world we are like him. There is no fear in love. But perfect love drives out fear, because fear has to do with punishment. The one who fears is not made perfect in love. (1 John 4:16–18)

Above all, love each other deeply, because love covers over a multitude of sins. (1 Peter 4:8)

This is how we know what love is: Jesus Christ laid down his life for us. And we ought to lay down our lives for our brothers. (1 John 3:16)

Good Communication

Whoever would love life and see good days must keep his tongue from evil and his lips from deceitful speech. He must turn from evil and do good; he must seek peace and pursue it. For the eyes of the Lord are on the righteous and his ears are attentive to their prayer. (1 Peter 3:10–12)

The good man brings good things out of the good stored up in his heart....For out of the overflow of his heart his mouth speaks. (Luke 6:45)

If I speak in the tongues of men and of angels, but have not love, I am only a resounding gong or a clanging cymbal. (1 Corinthians 13:1)

Do not let any unwholesome talk come out of your mouths, but only what is helpful for building others up according to their needs, that it may benefit those who listen. (Ephesians 4:29)

Unity

> My purpose is that they may be encouraged in heart and united in love, so that they may have the full riches of complete understanding, in order that they may know the mystery of God, namely, Christ, in whom are hidden all the treasures of wisdom and knowledge. (Colossians 2:2–3)

> Make every effort to keep the unity of the Spirit through the bond of peace. There is one body and one Spirit—just as you were called to one hope when you were called—one Lord, one faith, one baptism; one God and Father of all, who is over all and through all and in all. (Ephesians 4:3–6)

> May the God who gives endurance and encouragement give you a spirit of unity among yourselves as you follow Christ Jesus, so that with one heart and mouth you may glorify the God and Father of our Lord Jesus Christ. Accept one another, then, just as Christ accepted you, in order to bring praise to God. (Romans 15:5–7)

Big Gulps and Little Bites

There are many wonderful ways to find nourishment in God's Word. Some people enjoy reading through the entire Bible over the course of a year. Others like to take small pieces of the Word, chew on them for a while, and digest them slowly. There is no right or wrong method for studying the Bible. The important thing is to feed and find strength in God's Word on a regular basis.

You may want to consider joining a formal Bible study. Your church may offer group studies, or one or more of the churches in your area may host a national, nondenominational study program such as Bible Study Fellowship, Community Bible Study, or Precept upon

Precept. These programs offer systematic ways for studying God's Word in settings that welcome people of all backgrounds and levels of Bible knowledge.

No matter what method or venue you choose, Bible study ultimately comes down to your personal investigation and application of God's truth. I encourage you to meditate on Scripture daily and to ask God to open your eyes to see how you can apply his truth to your life. In my own experience, I have received great help and comfort in time of need through my study of the Bible. The words of Scripture have given me hope, joy, wisdom, and direction. One particular time the Word prepared me with peace. Let me explain.

On the morning of October 31, 1990, I received a phone call informing me that my mother had been hit by a car during her morning walk. The news came as a sudden shock. My mother was a healthy, vibrant, fifty-five-year-old woman who had never been hurt or seriously sick a day in her life! She took her daily walks on a safe neighborhood street. How could such a thing happen?

As my husband and I raced downtown through rush-hour traffic to get to the hospital, we had no idea how badly Mother had been hurt. I began to pray that the doctors would have wisdom, that Mother would feel comforted, and that she would not have any terrible complications or debilitating injuries.

To calm my anxious heart, I reached for the Bible in Curt's car. I opened it, seeking verses of comfort. I knew just where to go, because I had often found comfort there: the Book of Psalms. As I searched the pages, my eyes continually fell upon verses pointing to the glories of heaven and the blessings of dwelling eternally with the Lord:

> One thing I ask of the LORD, this is what I seek: that I may dwell in the house of the LORD all the days of my life, to gaze upon the beauty of the LORD and seek him in his temple. (Psalm 27:4)

Enter his gates with thanksgiving and his courts with praise. (Psalm 100:4)

Precious in the sight of the LORD is the death of his saints. (Psalm 116:15)

I didn't notice any verses that spoke of healing (although they abound)—only those that refer to being in the presence of the Lord. I said to Curt, "I think God is trying to tell me that Mother has died," and he agreed that I needed to be ready for that possibility. Until that moment I had not even considered that my mother might be gone; yet God was graciously preparing me through his Word, lovingly reminding me that heaven is the ultimate reward.

In fact, my precious mother had passed away. But I know I will see her again one day in heaven! She loved God's Word, and she taught her family to love it too. I'm so thankful for the powerful impact that Scripture continues to have in my life today. And I know it can have the same kind of impact in yours. Whether in a dramatic circumstance or through a day-by-day leading, God's Word is powerful and pertinent to the life of every positive wife.

As you read and meditate daily on God's Word, you will grow to know God in a deeper and more intimate way. You will glean wisdom and direction for life, and you will find comfort and hope for the journey. I think about the admonition God gave to Joshua as he assumed the role of leading the Israelites into the Promised Land: "Do not let this Book of the Law depart from your mouth; meditate on it day and night, so that you may be careful to do everything written in it. Then you will be prosperous and successful" (Joshua 1:8). That is our charge as positive wives: to mediate on God's Word day and night. That's the key to our success.

Blessed is the man who finds wisdom, the man who gains understanding, for she is more profitable than silver and yields better returns than gold. —Proverbs 3:13–14

She Knew the Secret

Generally speaking, beautiful and positive qualities don't simply show up in a person without some sort of internal or external motivation. You may remember that in an earlier chapter, I quoted the gifted author Catherine Marshall, who wrote about her decision to fast from criticism. Where did her motivation for spiritual growth come from? Her husband, Leonard LeSourd, wrote this about Catherine after she passed away:

> Bibles were scattered throughout our house…all editions, plus reference books and concordances. We often went to bed, turned out the light, and listened to a chapter of Scripture on tape….
>
> When upset or under spiritual assault or in physical pain, Catherine would go to her office, kneel by her chair, and open her Bible….She would read, then pray, then read, then pray some more….Catherine didn't read the Bible for solace or inspiration, but to have an encounter with the Lord….Catherine's passion for the Word permeated her whole life.[2]

According to Len, Catherine's deep love for God's Word was foundational to her life and to their life as a couple. It was the bottom line in all the family decisions they made together.

Could our husbands say about us what Len LeSourd wrote about his dear wife, Catherine? The truth is, God's Word is the secret to a positive life. May our pathways be lit by the light of his Word! May it be our foundation, our encouragement, our map for life! By giving us his living and eternal Word, God has given us great treasure. As Isaiah 40:8 says, "The grass withers and the flowers fall, but the word of our God stands forever." May we visit the treasure chest of the Bible each day and glean all the unfading riches it has to offer!

POWER POINT

⚙ **Read:** Proverbs 2. What are the benefits of wisdom mentioned in this chapter? Where does wisdom come from? (v. 6).

♡ **Pray:** O wise and holy Father, thank you for sharing your Word with us. Thank you for leading us and guiding us through your Word. The Scripture is truly a rich treasure. It is a wealth of wisdom and truth, encouragement, and love. Plant your words in my heart and allow them to grow into an abundant life filled with joy. Help me to be diligent to read your truth each day, and help my husband to see its value and desire it too. Open my eyes to the message you want me to learn. Please allow the wisdom from the Bible to make my marriage stronger, richer, and fuller. May I become a woman of your Word in all I say and do. In Jesus' name, amen.

💡 **Remember:** "All Scripture is God-breathed and is useful for teaching, rebuking, correcting and training in righteousness, so that the man of God may be thoroughly equipped for every good work" (2 Timothy 3:16–17).

☺ **Do:** Choose a book of the Bible to read, study, and meditate upon. Read a portion (several verses or a chapter) every day. Read it slowly and meditate on its truth. Ask God to teach you from his Word. Use a journal to record insights you receive or questions you have. Choose a verse from the passage to commit to memory.

Conclusion

Finish Strong!
Expecting the Best by Giving Your Best

Marriage is a lifelong process of discovering each other more deeply.

—Ingrid Trobisch

My daughter Grace runs on the cross-country team at school. During track season she works out with her teammates every morning at 6:00 A.M. Getting up so early to train takes discipline and hard work on her part, but it pays off in the races.

On Saturdays I go to the cross-country meets to cheer my daughter (and the rest of the team) on to victory. I stand at the starting gate to see the race begin; then once the girls are off and running, I find a spot near the finish line. I like to plant myself about fifty yards from the end, so I can give Grace and her teammates one last boost of encouragement as they pass by. The runners are tired, and their energy is expended at that point, but their finish is important.

Some of the runners slow down near the end; they're tired, and they're just hoping to make it to the finish line. Then there are other runners who see these last few yards as an opportunity to pour it on and pass their lagging competitors. Many runners improve their finish placement and time in the race during this last sprint. I love to cheer for all the girls on our school team as they come through the final stretch. My battle cry is simply, "Finish strong!" Sometimes that's all they need to hear to make one last push. "Yeah, pour it on!" I say. They have invested time, energy, and sweat to get this far, so why not make it the best race ever?

That's the same encouragement I send to you as you strive to be a positive wife. Finish strong! It's not easy. Marriage is a long-distance race—and it's uphill most of the way. Keep investing your 110 percent to make your marriage the best it can possibly be. I've heard it said many times, "A marriage may be made in heaven, but it takes a lot of work here on earth." And that's true. A good marriage does take continual work. We never get to the point where we can say, "Well, I've achieved all there is to achieve in my marriage. Now I'll just sit back and slide through the rest of life."

Singer Roberta Flack puts it this way: "Getting married is easy. Staying married is more difficult. Staying happily married for a lifetime should rank among the fine arts."[1] Does she make a happy, long-term marriage sound impossible? Don't worry. With God all things are possible! If God can make a blind man see, a lame man walk, and a dead man rise, then surely he can heal a hurting marriage or resurrect a dead relationship. The good news is, he is on this journey of marriage with us. He is our comfort, our strength, and our guide.

If It Is to Be...

Perhaps it would have been easier for you if I'd written this book to both you and your husband, telling each of you to give 110 percent to make your marriage everything it ought to be. But alas, this book is to you and other positive wives; and our charge is to give 110 percent to our marriages, whether our husbands do or not. Okay, okay—I'll try to find someone to write *The Power of a Positive Husband*. But while we're waiting, we still have the responsibility to love and respect our husbands unconditionally and to be positive influences in our marriages. You know as well as I do that husbands rarely read marriage books anyway!

In business my dad uses the phrase, "If it is to be, it is up to me"—ten little, two-letter words that pack a powerful punch! It's easy to make excuses or blame others for what happens in life. In marriage especially, we're tempted to waste time and energy blaming our husbands for our problems, disappointments, or challenges. Certainly a spouse may be a contributing factor in negative circumstances. But we can't answer for our husbands' actions; we can only answer for our own. We have a responsibility to make a positive contribution to our marriages and help them grow. The truth is, there are three players in a Christian marriage: the wife, the husband, and God. We need to do our part, allow God to do his part, and love and encourage our husbands to do their part.

I must be honest with you. I struggled in the writing of this book, because I'm vividly aware that I don't know about one crucial variable in your life: your husband. I don't know what he's like. I don't know where he stands with the Lord. I don't know if he is kind and loving, angry and inattentive, or somewhere in between. All I do know is that certain foundational truths can be applied to all of our lives as wives, and these are what I've presented in this book. It has been my desire to be sensitive to the variety of situations in which wives may find themselves, recognizing that additional counseling and intervention may be needed in certain situations.

I can't guarantee an easy ride if you follow the principles in this book. The only thing I know is that these seven principles for being a positive wife are powerful, not because I said so, but because they are based on biblical truth. The positive principles presented in these pages are found in the pages of God's Word. Being positive wives means we allow God to work in and through our lives and our marriages in a positive way.

I attended Baylor University in Waco, Texas—that's where Curt and I met. Our pet name for Baylor is "good ole BU." But those letters represent something different for positive wives: "Be you." Be yourself! Bring into your marriage the rich fullness of your talents, your gifts, your unique personality. Bring into your marriage a heart that is bent toward God. Grow spiritually in your personal walk with God, even if your husband doesn't. Be a positive influence for your family, even if your husband brings negatives. Be you! Be the best you that God created you to be. Don't give up or lose heart. Stay on the path he's put before you.

The apostle Peter spoke God's truth to the early Christians, and his words speak to us today as positive wives. Life was far from perfect for the first-century believers. Although they were doing what was right, they still suffered. It wasn't fair. Peter encouraged them not to whine or despair, but rather to be responsible for their own behavior in a positive way. Here's what he said in 1 Peter 3:8–17:

> Finally, all of you, live in harmony with one another; be sympathetic, love as brothers, be compassionate and humble. Do not repay evil with evil or insult with insult, but with blessing, because to this you were called so that you may inherit a blessing. For, "Whoever would love life and see good days must keep his tongue from evil and his lips from deceitful speech. He must turn from evil and do good; he must seek peace and pursue it. For the eyes of the Lord are on the righteous and his ears are attentive to their prayer, but the face of the Lord is against those who do evil."
>
> Who is going to harm you if you are eager to do good? But even if you should suffer for what is right, you are blessed. "Do not fear what they fear; do not be frightened." But in your hearts set apart Christ as Lord. Always be prepared to give an answer to everyone who asks you to give the reason for the hope that you have. But do this with gentleness and respect, keeping a clear conscience, so that those who speak maliciously against your good

behavior in Christ may be ashamed of their slander. It is better, if it is God's will, to suffer for doing good than for doing evil.

Let's determine to be a gift to our husbands and our marriages, allowing God to live and love through us. I know that sometimes no matter what a wife does right, a marriage may still have difficulties or even fall apart. But may it never be said of us that we are the problem! As much as possible, we must be the solution. Being a positive wife means being responsible for our own behavior, even when life isn't fair. It means giving all we can and then leaving the results to God. Being a positive wife is not about being perfect; it's about being faithful to be who God called us to be in our marriages.

They Carried Them

The story of the wives of Weinsberg, told in Bill Bennett's book *The Moral Compass*, reveals the fierce loyalty and commitment shown by a certain group of medieval wives toward their husbands and their marriages.

It happened in Germany, in the Middle Ages. The year was 1141. Wolf, the duke of Bavaria, sat trapped inside his castle of Weinsberg. Outside his walls lay the army of Frederick, the duke of Swabia, and his brother, the emperor Konrad.

The siege had lasted long, and the time had come when Wolf knew he must surrender. Messengers rode back and forth, terms were proposed, conditions allowed, arrangements completed. Sadly, Wolf and his officers prepared to give themselves to their bitter enemy.

But the wives of Weinsberg were not ready to lose all. They sent a message to Konrad, asking the emperor to promise safe conduct for all the women in the garrison, that they might come out with as many of their valuables as they could carry.

Where you start is not as important as where you finish. —Zig Ziglar

:)

263

The request was freely granted, and soon the castle gates opened. Out came the ladies—but in startling fashion. They carried not gold or jewels. Each one was bending under the weight of her husband, whom she hoped to save from the vengeance of the victorious host.

Konrad, who was really a generous and merciful man, is said to have been brought to tears by the extraordinary performance. He hastened to assure the women of their husbands' perfect safety and freedom. Then he invited them all to a banquet and made peace with the duke of Bavaria on terms much more favorable than expected.

The castle mount was afterwards known as the Hill of Weibertreue, or "woman's fidelity."[2]

What a powerful story of loyalty, love, faithfulness, resourcefulness, and strength! These women offer us an indelible picture of what it means to be a truly positive wife. We must learn from their example and show our own willingness to carry the weight of our marriages on our shoulders for parts of the journey when necessary. I'm not saying we should manipulate, push, or overpower our husbands. Rather, we must lift them up through the powerful, positive qualities of:

- Love
- Commitment
- Respect
- Encouragement
- Physical attraction
- Responsibility
- Spiritual strength

As we develop in each of these areas, God's Word can begin to work powerfully within us, and our marriages can turn into great blessings for both partners. May our battle cry be Galatians 6:9: "Let us not become weary in doing good, for at the proper time we will reap a harvest if we do not give up." And may God use each of us in a powerful way to make a positive difference in our marriages.

Enjoy the journey and finish strong!

POWER POINT

⚙ **Read:** Colossians 1. Notice Paul's prayer for the Colossians in verses 9–14. I want you to know that I stopped typing just now and prayed this prayer for you, dear reader. Will you take a moment to pray it for your husband? After reading the first chapter of Colossians, make a list of the qualities you see there that could describe a positive wife.

♡ **Pray:** Dear and precious heavenly Father, I praise you that you are the God above all Creation, and yet you choose to give love, power, and strength to me! Thank you for caring for me, helping me, and guiding me along this pathway of life. Bless my marriage. Help me to be a positive influence in my marriage. Help me to lift my husband up and be a complement to him all the days of our lives. Take my meager yet faithful gifts and abilities and use them to be a blessing in our home. May my words and actions be a joyful testimony to a life lived for your glory. In Jesus' name I pray, amen.

♡ **Remember:** "His divine power has given us everything we need for life and godliness through our knowledge of him who called us by his own glory and goodness" (2 Peter 1:3).

☺ **Do:** Take a highlighter and go back through the pages of this book, marking those passages that have made the greatest impact on your heart and mind. Write the memory verses from each chapter on index cards, and if you haven't already done so, begin to memorize them. As you carry God's Word in your heart, you will find that it assists you along life's journey, giving you direction, nourishment, and strength to be a positive wife.

Notes

Introduction: The Influence of a Positive Wife

1. S. M. Henriques, *God Can Handle It...Marriage* (Nashville: Brighton Books, 1998), 78.

Chapter 1: Wifeology

1. Scott Kim, *Bogglers* (www.discover.com: Discover, Vol. 22 No. 3, March 2001).

2. Gary L. Thomas, *Authentic Faith* (Grand Rapids: Zondervan, 2002), 27.

3. John Blanchard, ed., *More Gathered Gold* (Hertfordshire, England: Evangelical Press, 1986), 199.

4. Edward Rowell and Bonne Steffen, ed., *Humor for Preaching and Teaching* (Grand Rapids: Baker Books, 1996), 183.

Chapter 2: It's Not about You!

1. Walter B. Knight, *Knight's Master Book of 4000 Illustrations* (Grand Rapids: Eerdmans Publishing, 1956), 478.

2. Blanchard, *More Gathered Gold*, 223.

3. Robert Foster and James Bryan Smith, *Devotional Classics* (New York: Renovare, Inc., 1993), 47.

4. Ibid., 82.

5. Joyce Brown, *Courageous Christians* (Chicago: Moody Press, 2000), 111–12.

6. Henriques, *God...Marriage*, 33.

Chapter 3: The Truth about True Love

1. C. S. Lewis, *The Four Loves* (New York: Harcourt Brace Jovanovich, 1960), 87.
2. Glenn Van Ekeren, *Speaker's Sourcebook II* (Englewood Cliffs, N.J.: Prentice Hall, 1994), 313.

Chapter 4: The Truest Joy and the Toughest Journey

1. Selwyn Crawford, "Ten Years Later, Shots Still Echo in Courthouse Halls" *Dallas Morning News,* July 1, 2002, 1A, 8A.
2. *God's Little Devotional Book for Couples* (Tulsa, Okla.: Honor Books, 1995), 70.
3. Evangelical Press News Service, reprinted in *Fresh Illustrations for Preaching & Teaching,* Edward K. Rowell, ed. (Grand Rapids: Baker Book House, 1997), 76–77.
4. Knight, *4,000 Illustrations,* 230.

Chapter 5: A Rare Commodity

1. Aimee Howd, "Smart Plan to Save Marriages," *Insight on the News* (March 29, 1999), 14.
2. *American Quotations,* Gorton Carruth and Eugene Ehrlich, ed. (New York: Gramercy Books, 1988), 558.
3. Ibid., 561.
4. Gary Thomas, *Sacred Marriage* (Grand Rapids: Zondervan, 2000). The quote is actually the subtitle of the book.
5. John M. Gottman and Nan Silver, *The Seven Principles for Making Marriage Work* (New York: Crown, 1999), 21.
6. Daniel B. Baker, *Power Quotes* (www.MotivationalQuotes.com).

Chapter 6: The Art of Arguing

1. "Marriage After All These Years," a pamphlet distributed by The Christophers, 12 East 48th Street, New York 10017.
2. Ellen Fein and Sherrie Schneider, *The Rules for Marriage* (New York: Warner Books, 2001), 81.
3. Ekeren, *Speaker's Sourcebook II,* 357.
4. Jean Lush, *Women and Stress* (Grand Rapids: Fleming H. Revell, 1992), 109–12.
5. Bob Phillips, *Great Thoughts and Funny Sayings* (Wheaton, Ill.: Tyndale House Publishers, 1993), 320.
6. Henriques, *God...Marriage,* 100.

Chapter 7: His Secret Desire

1. Kati Marton, *Hidden Power* (New York: Pantheon Books, 2001), 353.
2. Zig Ziglar, *Zig* (New York: Doubleday, 2002).

Chapter 8: Attitude Is Everything

1. Robert Louis Stevenson, *A Child's Garden of Verses* (New York: Delacorte Press, 1985), 31.

2. Amy Steedman, *When They Were Children* (Edinburgh, England: Ballantyne, Hanson & Co., n.d.), 382.

3. Ekeren, *Speaker's Sourcebook II*, 47.

4. Abigail Van Buren, "Dear Abby" (Universal Press Syndicate), *Dallas Morning News*, August 14, 2002, 4C.

5. Ken Blanchard and S. Truett Cathy, *The Generosity Factor* (Grand Rapids: Zondervan, 2002).

6. This information comes from an e-mail posted on June 11, 2002 by Jody Crain, field chairman of New Tribes Mission in the Philippines. Jody was one of the first people to visit Gracia in the hospital after she'd been rescued and evacuated.

7. Helen Hosier, *One Hundred Christian Women Who Changed the Twentieth Century* (Grand Rapids: Fleming H. Revell, 2000), 350.

8. Ibid., 355.

9. Ibid., 356–57.

Chapter 9: What If He Doesn't Deserve It?

1. Bill and Lynne Hybels, *Fit to Be Tied* (Grand Rapids: Zondervan , 1991), 63.

2. Henriques, *God…Marriage*, 121.

3. Ibid., 123.

4. Leslie Vernick, *How to Act Right When Your Spouse Acts Wrong* (Colorado Springs: WaterBrook Press, 2001), 34.

Chapter 10: Word Power Made Easy

1. Roy B. Zuck, *The Speakers Quote Book* (Grand Rapids: Kregel Publications, 1997), 129.

2. Ibid., 129.

3. *God's Little Devotional Book for Couples* (Tulsa, Okla.: Honor Books, 2001), 20–21.

4. Catherine Marshall, *A Closer Walk* (Old Tappan, N.J.: Chosen Books/Revell, 1986), 102–104.

5. Zuck, *The Speaker's Quote Book*, 128.

Chapter 11: Extraordinary Companionship

1. Quote used by permission from Pastor Pete Briscoe, Bent Tree Bible Fellowship, Carrollton, Texas.

2. Leil Lowndes, *How to Make Anyone Fall in Love with You* (Chicago: Contemporary Books, 1996), 106.

Chapter 12: Beauty Inside Out

1. Nancy Stafford, *Beauty by the Book* (Sisters, Oreg.: Multnomah Publishers, 2002), 19.
2. Ibid., 11.
3. Marilyn Vos Savant, "The Intelligence Report," *Parade Magazine,* June 17, 2001.
4. William T. Clower, *The Fat Fallacy: Applying the French Diet to the American Lifestyle* (North Versailles, Pa.: Perusal Press, 2001).
5. Gary Smalley, *Food and Love* (Wheaton, Ill.: Tyndale House, 2001), 41.

Chapter 13: Sensational Sex

1. Henriques, *God...Marriage,* 130.
2. Kevin Leman, *Becoming a Couple of Promise* (Colorado Springs: NavPress, 1999), 97.
3. Henriques, *God...Marriage,* 131.
4. Ibid., 130.
5. Ibid., 132.
6. Lowell D. Streiker, ed., *Nelson's Big Book of Laughter* (Nashville: Thomas Nelson Publishers, 2000), 389.
7. Joan Declaire, "Your Marriage Getting Better," *Reader's Digest,* February 2003, 68.
8. Henriques, *God...Marriage,* 132.
9. Knight, *4,000 Illustrations,* 399.

Chapter 14: Yours, Mine, and Ours

1. Mary Stark, *What No One Tells the Bride* (New York: Hyperion, 1998), 113.
2. Curt Ladd, *The Survivor's Handbook* (Dallas: First Financial Publications, 1993), 130–32. Reprinted with permission from the author.

Chapter 15: Domestic Diva

1. *Life Application Bible,* New Living Translation (Wheaton, Ill.: Tyndale House Publishers, 1996), 1022.
2. Peggy Anderson, ed., *Great Quotes from Great Women* (Lombard, Ill.: Celebrating Excellence Publishing Co., 1992), 114.

Chapter 16: Intimate Fellowship

1. Blanchard, *More Gathered Gold,* 232.
2. Ibid., 232.
3. Ibid., 233.

4. John Stott, *The Letters of John,* published within the *Tyndale New Testament Commentaries,* revised edition (Leicester, England: InterVarsity Press; Grand Rapids: Eerdmans, 1988), 188.

5. Knight, *4,000 Illustrations,* 491.

Chapter 17: God's Love Letters

1. Dr. Paul R. Fink, *The New Open Bible* (Nashville: Thomas Nelson Publishers, 1990), 25.

2. *God's Little Devotional Book for Couples* (Tulsa, Okla.: Honor Books, 2001), 48–49.

Conclusion: Finish Strong!

1. Henriques, *God...Marriage,* 138.

2. William J. Bennett, *The Moral Compass* (New York: Simon & Schuster, 1996), 510.